THE POZZY

A HISTORY OF LEDBURY PRESERVES

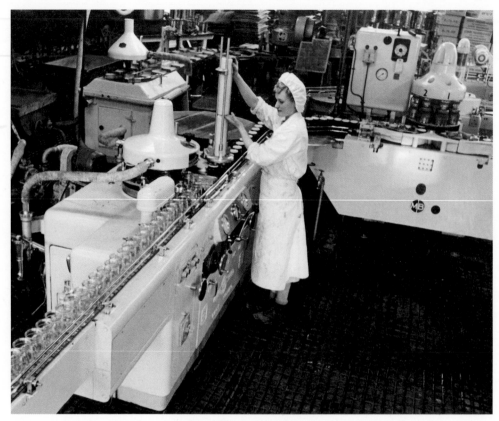

Jam from steriliser entering filling, capping and sealing line, early 1960s

The Pozzy

A History of

LEDBURY PRESERVES

Brian Hudson ～ Ken Jollans ～ David Smith

MUNTJAC PRESS

Published in 2008 by
Muntjac Press Limited
Ledbury, Herefordshire, UK
www.muntjacpress.com

ISBN-13 978-0-9548305-4-0
ISBN-10 0-9548305-4-7

Designed and typeset in Arno Pro and Optima
at Five Seasons Press, Hereford
and printed on 75% recycled paper
by Cambrian Printers
Aberystwyth SY23 3TN

CONTENTS

Introduction

When Premier Foods, the new owner of Ledbury Preserves, decided in 2007 to close the site it signalled the end of a rich history of jam production at the factory on Little Marcle Road. For many years, the company had produced some of the very finest quality preserves for retail customers and food manufacturers alike, as well as venturing at various stages in its history into the production of fruit juice, cider and latterly suet. As the number of preserves factories in the UK declined over the years, the Ledbury business stood out as a model of efficiency and profitability. Prior to the decision to close the factory, it could credibly claim to be both the most profitable large scale preserves business in the country and the producer of the best marmalades and some of the very best quality conserves anywhere in the world. It was also the largest producer of retail mincemeat and the only producer of shredded suet in the world. Now, only the production of suet remains, produced by the new occupiers of the site on behalf of Premier Foods.

The decision to close the factory was no reflection on the performance of the company or the skills of the people who worked there. Premier's decision, consistent with its overall strategy, aimed to achieve maximum efficiency through scale by consolidating its jam production into the Histon factory in Cambridgeshire. This involved the closures in swift succession of not only the Ledbury factory but also its sister factory in Manchester and the Chivers factory in Dublin which Premier had acquired at around the same time. These closures, following hard on the heels of the closure of the Fruitfield marmalade factory in Dublin in early 2007, meant that the number of large scale preserves factories in the British Isles was halved within little more than a year.

The history of Ledbury Preserves is a rich one. It includes bankruptcy, intrigue, high and low finance, colourful personal rivalries and occasional fraud. It is a story of great competence interspersed with episodes of manifest incompetence. This book is no hagiography. It has been researched and written by a group of people both inside and outside the business working for enjoyment and not dancing to any particular tune, and it has been privately commissioned and published. Nevertheless, we have taken care to maintain respect for the people who have worked in the business and the revelations included herein are unlikely to trouble the Sunday newspapers. For all that, it is an interesting story and one which deserves to be told.

When we started this project, we expected that the closure of the factory in the summer of 2008 would be followed by a period of inactivity on the site on Little Marcle Road. This turned out to be very wide of the mark. The sale of the site to Universal Beverages Ltd in December 2007 marked the beginning of what we hope will be a whole new story, which may be waiting to be told 100 years from now. Where for many decades, local apples were turned into jam, apples from the same orchards—if not from the same trees—will now be milled for cider production. The loss of employment opportunities in one industry is being countered, at least partially, by new openings in another industry. And who knows, just as Ledbury Preserves once had a dabble at making cider, years from now Universal Beverages or someone else may consider making jam there once again. But for now, this book tells the story of how large scale jam production started in Ledbury, and how it ended.

1 ⤳ The Roots of the Company

Before the Beginning

Most people simply knew it as 'The Jam Factory'. Occasionally, and more bizarrely, it was also called 'The Pozzy'. No one knows where this strange alternative name came from, but it was fairly common parlance in post-war years and probably started long before that. But 'The Jam Factory' will do. That was the name most people used—and not just those who worked there; everyone in Ledbury knew exactly what was meant if the jam factory was mentioned.

And everyone knew where it was. It was out to the west of the town, on the other side of the by-pass. But that road, curling round the edge of Ledbury, is a newcomer; the jam factory had been there for several generations before the by-pass was even thought about—and everyone throughout those generations knew what the jam factory was, and where it was.

In the early days, it might have been described as being well out of the town—across the river and on a bit. Not by the hop fields to the north of the town, but west, next to Fairtree Farm and its orchards. From the road between the farm and the factory, you could make out the spire of St Michael's Church, seen over the rooftops of Newtown and Happy Land as the areas up Bridge Street were known. And sometimes too, you might see the smoke, and hear the sound—or even the whistle—of a short passenger train as it puffed its way from Dymock up to the Town Halt station, before struggling up the incline to the main junction station next to the abattoir on the Homend.

Perhaps inevitably in such a long life, it has had several different names over the door. In 80 or so years, changes of ownership were unavoidable. To the people dealing with company records, these changes were important and they were certainly critical in determining the shape and prosperity (or otherwise) of the company itself. But to everyone in Ledbury—to those who worked there, to those who lived in the town—it remained The Jam Factory.

Jam and bricks may seem strange bedfellows but before jam was made there it was a brickworks, run by a local farmer, John Davies.

One source suggests that, in the 1850s and 1860s, these brickworks were

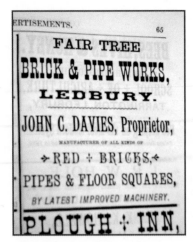

*Advert from 1885 for
John Davies's brickworks*

owned by Robert Ballard but there is room for serious doubt on that score. If Ballard did own it, then it played a crucial role in the development of Ledbury since it would have been bricks from this site—five million of them—that were used in the construction of a key landmark of the town—the railway viaduct. Robert's brother, Stephen, was the engineer responsible for the building of the Worcester-Hereford railway and when he needed bricks for the viaduct, he kept it in the family with Robert's brickworks being used for their production. It is an impressive structure in true Victorian grandeur—it has 31 arches, is 330 yards long and more than 60 feet high.

However, John Davies's descendants are unaware of any Ballard connection and had always believed that John himself had set up the brickworks at Fairtree, while the Ballard family have always understood that Robert's brickworks were in New Street and not on the Fairtree Farm site—something other records would tend to confirm.

Certainly by the 1880s, both Fairtree Farm and a brick and tile works opposite were run by John Davies. The Davies family leased this land which was part of the massive Upper Hall Estate: a 1910 land assessment confirms that even then the occupier was 'J C Davies', while the owner is shown as 'W A N Martin'. The Martins were one of Ledbury's grand families and had owned Upper Hall since marrying into the Skyppes (another such grand family) in 1812.

John Charles Davies was a local man, born in Tarrington in 1856. He was on the Ledbury Council and became a JP but was also—and for this story, more importantly—what we would today call an entrepreneur. He acquired considerable tracts of land, stretching from Fairtree across to Pixley in one direction and towards Leadington in the other. While at Fairtree Farm, he began an extensive rebuilding of Hill House (on the Ledbury to Ross Road), ensuring there was a room for each of his 15 children. The house also had an early form of central heating and was one of the first in the town to have its own telephone—the number being 'Ledbury 4'. Moving-in day was 1899 and the family walked across the fields from Fairtree, carrying the tables and chairs from the old home to the new!

John Davies was a man fascinated by new inventions and, for example, he is credited with his home being the first building in Ledbury to have electric light. *The Ledbury Free Press* of 22 November 1892 announced this 'honour' as in the illustration opposite.

Although the 'safety bicycle' was not patented until the mid 1880s, so starting the phase-out of the old penny-farthing, the Davies family all had these newfangled machines soon after—and a camera to record the fact. In the photograph below from around 1900, John Davies is on the far left, while his eldest son Tom—who will be a key player in the story of the jam factory—is second from the right.

We have this week to announce the first instance of the public use of the electric light in the parish of Ledbury. To Mr J.C. Davies, of the Fair Tree Farm and Brickworks, just on the border of the town, must be awarded the honour of thus introducing to our midst what plainly will be the light of the future.

Ledbury Free Press, November 22, 1892.

Apart from farming which, ostensibly, was his main occupation, by the 1880s John was running the brickworks across the road from Fairtree. Every brick had his name imprinted on it—and the railways do feature in the story here,

since his bricks were used in the construction of the Ledbury to Gloucester branch line which opened in 1885 and, sadly, closed to passenger traffic in 1959.

By the end of the First World War, however, bricks had been replaced by preserves.

The Start Of It All

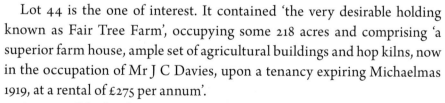

On 17 June 1919, there was an auction at the Feathers Hotel in Ledbury's High Street. The Upper Hall estate was selling (in a series of separate lots) some 1500 acres of 'exceptionally productive and well watered' agricultural land including 'four residences, two smallholdings, five farms, corn mill, business premises, cottages, building sites and standing timber'.

Lot 44 is the one of interest. It contained 'the very desirable holding known as Fair Tree Farm', occupying some 218 acres and comprising 'a superior farm house, ample set of agricultural buildings and hop kilns, now in the occupation of Mr J C Davies, upon a tenancy expiring Michaelmas 1919, at a rental of £275 per annum'.

As part of the lot, however, attention was drawn to 'the well known jam factory [which] has been carried on here for some time past by Mr T E Davies, affording a ready market for the farm fruit at best prices'. It added that 'the factory buildings belong to the tenant, the site having been agreed

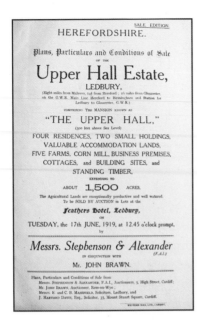

to be let to him for a term of ten years from 29 September 1915, at a rental of £10 per annum for the first five years, and thereafter at a rental of £15 per annum'.

Who bought the farm at this point is not clear. By 1919, John Davies was not living there, having turned his interest over to another of his sons. That did not stop him from attending the auction nor, it seems from trying to influence the proceedings. The auctioneer commented to him that 'you have made speeches today about the injustices you are suffering, but now it transpires that you are not suffering any injustices at all because you are not the tenant'. John Davies tried to defend himself on the grounds that he was speaking on behalf of the tenant, but the auctioneer stopped this line of argument, saying that 'if everybody who are not tenants came forward and made speeches, I do not know where we would be'.

Bidding by members of the Davies family reached £7,000 but the auctioneer refused to sell it at that price and withdrew the property. However, the jam factory continued to operate under the lease signed in 1915, and the implication from a different source document is that John Davies was subsequently to acquire the Fairtree Farm estate.

Born in 1883, Mr T E Davies—Tom—was the eldest son of John Davies and was a real chip off the old block. He had his fingers in a large number of pies—something that was to bring him grief a little later on—and there were often strong differences of opinion between him and his father. He was also to be married three times and divorced twice—something not done lightly in those times.

What had happened prior to the 1919 auction and more importantly, what happened subsequently, is complex and confusing and can certainly rival the machinations of any business transaction in today's world. However, the idea of a jam factory did not happen suddenly.

In December 1903, one of the Davies family, probably John, gave a talk at the Ledbury Reading Room and Library under the title 'Fruit Culture' and in which he suggested starting a cider factory, a jam factory and a general depot for fruits. By 1905, Ledbury had a cider company, though it is not known where, or whether John Davies had any hand in it, but given his dynamic nature, it is perhaps not surprising that a jam factory was to follow in due course.

In 1906 and 1907, Tom—then in his early twenties—farmed Pixley Court for his father; this property was then owned by Lord Somers' Eastnor estate. (Pixley Court still stands and is on the Ledbury side of what is now the A4172, the road from Trumpet to Preston Cross and Dymock. From there, it would have been a relatively short walk across the fields to Fairtree Farm.) After two years, his father gave him £2,000 worth of stock and Tom became the tenant at a rent of £267 10s per annum, and began to farm it on his own account.

Tom Davies 1906–7

In 1916, Pixley Court Farm was put up for sale by Lord Somers and Tom bought it for around £4,600—different sources give marginally different figures. Not content with acquiring Pixley Court, Tom started a new venture in the same year: a jam factory at the Fairtree Farm site in Ledbury. Initially known as the Pixley Court Jam Works, this business was later to

become T E Davies Ltd and, later still, Ledbury Preserves Ltd.

This, however, was almost certainly not Tom's first jam making business. A case can be made for suggesting that either earlier, or in parallel with the Fairtree Farm operation, Tom was making jam at Pixley Court itself, a possibility to be considered in more detail later in this chapter. Whether he did or did not make jam at Pixley, he most certainly did have a jam making business at another site altogether at Withington, near Hereford.

The Withington site's principal trade was not jam making but tile making. Officially, this was the Lugwardine Tile Works of Godwin & Sons and was immediately adjacent to Withington Railway Station. Founded in the mid 1800s by William Godwin, the company had passed to his son William Henry in 1883 and had a high reputation, having produced paving tiles for over 300 churches and other public buildings, including Pershore Abbey and the Manchester Assize Courts. Although inheriting a very successful going concern, William Henry was no tile maker and the business slowly declined. In 1906, it was bought out by another company which had little more success; in 1912, it was again advertised for sale and this time it was bought for £8,500 by Tom Davies. Tom continued to make tiles there but part of the factory was used to produce jams, pickles and bottled fruits and may have made the jars as well. In the longer term, Tom did not succeed where others had failed and by 1927 the tile works was in liquidation.

The Withington jam factory did not survive, nor did anything that may have been at Pixley. For now, the story of Tom Davies's jam making ventures will concentrate on the Ledbury site, this being the factory that was to out-live any others, and to survive for the following 92 years. By 1919, when the Fair Tree Farm site was up for auction, the jam factory there was clearly well established. Indeed, by 1920, it was sufficiently well known for the Ledbury telephone exchange list to have an entry which simply read:

Davies, T E, Jam Factory 48

Although known as the Jam Factory, fruit preserving and bottling were also key lines of business, with almost any obtainable fruit being processed. In 1918, for example, Tom Davies was advertising that '100 tons of rhubarb [was] wanted at Pixley Court Jam Works, Ledbury', while a year later he was saying that 'T E Davies is a buyer of all kinds of jam fruits' with 'best prices given' and that fruit would be 'received at Ledbury and Withington'. At first sight, it may be a little hard to understand how or why a jam factory was established in the middle of the war. As early as August 1914, shortages of goods were being expected and grocers were giving due warning to their customers that due to 'the grave situation in Europe, we can offer nothing firm'. By 1918, a government licence was needed to deal in wholesale supplies of jam, with maxi-mum prices for the finished product being set by someone described as 'The Food Controller'. However, there would have been a great need for home-produced foods for the domestic market and jam making would have been seen as a good way of using surplus fruit from local farms, not least from Tom Davies's own orchards at Pixley Court.

Although there was no conscription at that time, find-ing labour to work the local farms and the factory itself would have been difficult. As early as 1915, fruit growers were expressing their anxiety at the lack of men available to harvest the crop, and noting that ladies were 'volunteer-ing' to take on this work.

It was against this background that in September 1916, Tom Davies was in the local police court trying to defend

Advert from Tilley's Almanac, 1920

an Irishman, William Young, who was charged under the Military Service Act with being an absentee from the forces. The defence hinged on the fact that Young was Tom's greatly needed jam boiler! Tom Davies offered to stand bail 'for any amount the bench liked to fix' since without this person, his business was at a standstill. He added that 'we have over a ton of plums and if they are not boiled tomorrow, they will have to be thrown to the pigs'. No doubt wary of this offer, the magistrate fixed the bail at £50 but after consideration, Tom Davies said 'in that case, the defendant had better remain in custody.' The case continued in the Herefordshire Appeals Tribunal the following month, by which time Tom advanced a new argument: that he 'had a large contract to supply troops'.

Troops may not have been the only people he was supplying. His family are sure that Tom was awarded a contract to supply jams to Buckingham Palace and as such, was allowed to put the royal crest on his jam jar labels. It is not clear when this occurred, nor whether the jam involved came from Ledbury, Withington or (later) from what was to be his new home at Webton Court.

As an aside, pleading for his jam boiler was not the only time in 1916 that Tom Davies appeared in court. In July of that year, he should have appeared at Worcester City Police Court, charged with failing to produce his licence while driving a car and driving 'using headlights'. The court was also told that, during this episode, Tom had driven his car at a policeman who was trying to note the number plate. Tom did not turn up for the proceedings, where it was stated that he already had several convictions, both for driving offences and for assault.

Despite labour shortages, there were clearly some good harvests in the war years. In June 1918, the local paper—then called the Ledbury Guardian—reported that 'Ledbury was favoured on Tuesday with a large motor van full of pots of jam for sale. The van came from a neighbouring town and stood in the market place and appeared to be doing very good business in the plum and apple line at controlled prices. At the same time, it does not seem the thing for these people to be allowed to come and sell in the streets without paying any rates and taxes and in direct opposition to the tradesmen who have heavy rates, taxes and wages to pay.'

Two months later, prices and transport were in the paper's spotlight. 'The maximum price for blackberries on and after Wednesday of this week is to be 3d a pound to the pickers if they sell them to the retail shops for resale, or 4½d a pound if they sell them to the jam factory. The higher price paid by the jam factory is to encourage the public to sell them to the factory instead of the shops—the height of absurdity as I heard one townsman remark. Here in Ledbury town, the district is deluged with blackberries and is sending tons away every day, yet at the same time a large consignment of blackberries came to Ledbury station for the local jam factory right from Bewdley. This is how the authorities are saving the transport of the country!'

As the war drew to an end, Tom Davies's ventures—both personal and business—continued at full speed. There was jam making at Ledbury, Withington and possibly Pixley, and tile making at the Withington site. In 1919, he expanded his farming interests by purchasing the 200 acres of Poolend Farm, just across the main road from Pixley Court. He moved to live at Poolend, selling off a considerable quantity of household furniture from Pixley Court in the process. He was later to say that around 1919, he was worth £40,000—a very considerable sum at that time.

If Tom Davies had stuck with just his farm at Pixley Court and the jam factory, the subsequent story might have been very different, but he had great ambitions and was starting to overstretch himself considerably. Within a relatively short space of time the bubble was to burst. Tom was to be in the bankruptcy court and Ledbury Preserves would enter a new phase in its history.

Bankruptcy

1928 did not start well for Tom Davies. On Monday 9 January in that year, he faced his first public examination in the Hereford bankruptcy court.

Matters had been building to a head for some time with a series of complicated deals to try to head off his problems, but to no avail. By 1926, both the Lugwardine tile works at Withington and the Ledbury jam factory had been running into financial difficulties, and his personal property dealings confused matters further. He had, as he readily admitted in court, 'too many irons in the fire'. He told the court that he estimated his losses in the tile works at £15,000 and in Ledbury Preserves at £30,000. Both companies had by that time gone into receivership.

Inevitably, the whole sorry story had started much earlier than this and is a confused mélange of financial transactions involving his businesses and his personal life. Business loans were backed by personal guarantees which, in the event, were to be called in. Although life looked good in 1919, it is to that year that the root of Tom Davies's troubles can be traced. He had bought the Poolend property then for £9,000 with a £5,000 mortgage. However, there was then a second mortgage on Poolend given to the Dressler Tunnel Oven Company for £4,200 to cover the cost of purchasing a tunnel oven needed at the Lugwardine Tile Works. So started the chain of events that was to unravel a few years later.

In the meantime, things did not seem too bad. In February 1920, the company of T E Davies Ltd had been formed 'to carry on the business of fruit bottlers and manufacturers of jams, marmalade etc.' that Tom Davies was already running—with its registered offices given as Withington. While there was a nominal capital of £100,000, just two £1 shares were issued, one held by Tom Davies himself and the other by his Birmingham solicitor, Francis Pepper. In the following year, the company itself took on the lease of the Fairtree Farm factory site but this time, leasing it from John Davies for £45 per year; it is this reference that led to the earlier assumption that by this time, John Davies owned the land.

Within a couple of years, however, Tom Davies was finding himself over-stretched financially. With two farms (Pixley Court and Poolend), the Ledbury jam factory, mounting debts and pressures from the Lugwardine Tile Works, he was feeling the need for ready money.

In 1923, he had put both Pixley Court and the 'Pixley Court Jam Factory' up for auction but both properties were withdrawn when bidding did not reach the reserve prices of £25,000 for the farm and £5,000 for the factory. By 1925, however, he ended up selling both Pixley Court and Poolend to one of his brothers, Harry, for £23,500. Despite all this and the increasing problems at Lugwardine, in 1925 he still went ahead and bought another farm and property for himself—Webton Court at Kingstone on the other side of Hereford. He was later to admit in the bankruptcy court that this was something he should never have done. Webton Court cost him £11,500; he found £4,500 of this in cash but raised the balance on yet more mortgages.

It was the year in between these two events—1924—that saw some important changes in the ownership and management of the Ledbury jam factory. Having failed to sell the business at auction the previous year, some of the hitherto nominal shares became a reality, with 1,000 £1 shares being issued and divided equally between four grocery concerns from different towns in South Wales, with each of these shareholders also becoming a director. It is not possible at this distance to know the reasons for bringing in external directors; it may have been part of a strategy to involve retail outlets in the jam making business and so secure markets, or it may simply have been a way of raising capital, or perhaps a mix of the two.

In August 1924, as part of this management re-organisation, the company name was changed from 'T E Davies Ltd' to 'Ledbury Preserves Ltd', with its registered offices becoming simply 'The Works, Ledbury. In the following month—September 1924—the process went a stage further, and an agreement was reached between Tom Davies ('the vendor') and Ledbury Preserves ('the company') whereby 'the vendor will sell and the company will purchase the business of the vendor as a going concern and also the leasehold premises belonging to the vendor and situate at Ledbury'. In return for selling out in this way, Tom Davies received £100 in cash, 4,500 preference and 2,450 ordinary £1 shares; he was, though, to remain a director of the company for the time being.

1926 and 1927 were to be crunch years all round. Firstly, in 1926, things had reached breaking point at the Lugwardine tile works and matters looked so bad that the bank (which held some two-thirds of the company's debenture shares) appointed a receiver. An Order was subsequently made in the High Court for a compulsory winding-up of the company. The Dressler company, wanting its money for the oven, started to sue Tom Davies personally for just over £2,000.

Things were not going well either for Ledbury Preserves. In January 1926, the company secured its monies on a debenture with the Ledbury branch of Lloyd's Bank. It was also in that year that Tom Davies was not re-elected as a director of the company. In the summer of 1927 the jam factory re-mortgaged the property and issued a debenture of £6,000 to the Midland Bank, paying off the Lloyd's liabilities in doing so.

At the start of 1927, Tom's personal finances were worsening and his ordinary shares in the company (now with an estimated value of just £300) were transferred to his solicitor as security for debts and interest which, together, were estimated at £650. Matters worsened, and by November of that year, he cancelled the whole of his own preference shares in return for a payment of £625, this also being passed to his solicitor to cover other loans which had been made to him. Even this was not enough and again, in November 1927 Webton Court was sold and he was left, with his two sons, simply to manage the farm for someone else for the unprincely sum of £6 a week.

Around this time, Tom Davies was going through the first of his two divorces and it has been a long-held family belief that his bankruptcy was a smoke screen to reduce any divorce settlement he might face. The case took down not just Tom, but his brother Harry as well, and caused a great deal of upset and illness in the family. Tom had undoubtedly created a vortex of complex cross-financial transactions affecting both his business and personal life, which were hard to untangle and which were to change the course of the Ledbury Preserves story.

When his preference shares in Ledbury Preserves had been sold in late 1927, a condition agreed with the company was that the other directors should raise £3,000 in cash to help the company, but they did not do this. A financial crisis existed at the jam factory and the bank (which held the debenture shares) called in the receivers to run the company and investigate its future financial viability.

This was the end of Tom Davies's involvement with Ledbury Preserves. His personal affairs were in chaos and he was in the bankruptcy court. He told the court that he had also done a considerable amount of Stock Exchange speculation which had been profitable, as had apparently, his farming activities—something which surprised the Official Receiver given that so many other farmers had lost money. All in all, he told the court that his liabilities were around £6,000 but his assets just £285.

There had, indeed, been too many irons in the fire and it was time for Tom Davies to bow out of the Ledbury Preserves story—except for one last intriguing and almost unanswerable question: did the jam factory story actually start at Pixley Court rather than Ledbury?

The Pixley Connection

There has long been a suggestion that Tom Davies's first jam factory was not in Ledbury itself, but on his Pixley Court property. There is some evidence for this, but it is not totally conclusive. If there was a factory at Pixley, this raises a number of other perplexing questions and it is unlikely now that the question will ever be fully answered.

The case for Pixley Court starts with a long held belief in the area that jam was made there, possibly fuelled by the business's original name of the Pixley Court Jam Works. The large quantity of broken glass jam jars found under the topsoil on parts of the estate strengthens this belief.

There is certainly no dispute as to the name. The Pixley Court Jam Works is on record as an accepted name from the outset. However, in the 1928 reports of Tom Davies's bankruptcy, it is stated quite explicitly that in 1916, he 'commenced the Pixley Court Jam Works, afterwards called the Ledbury Preserves'. There is no suggestion that he started the jam factory before 1916 nor that the Pixley Works and Ledbury Preserves are anything other than one and the same business.

This statement and timing ties in well with the fact that in late 1915, Tom Davies took a ten year lease on part of the Fairtree Farm estate in Ledbury and that by the time of the 1919 Fairtree auction, reference is made to 'the well known jam factory [which] has been carried on here for some time past'. If there was a separate factory at Pixley, either before or after 1916, there was no reference to it in these auction papers or at the 1928 bankruptcy hearing.

A more significant point comes in 1923 when Tom Davies put both Pixley Court and 'the lease, goodwill, plant and machinery of the Pixley Jam Factory' up for auction. It may therefore be thought surprising that—if it were the Ledbury site being sold—it is still referred to as the 'Pixley Jam Factory' (though not, it should be noted, as the Pixley Court Factory). Use of the Pixley name may, though, have simply been a marketing ploy. Consider these three points:

First, the name of 'Ledbury Preserves' had not been registered in 1923; the company was officially trading as T E Davies Ltd, so reverting to an earlier colloquial name may have made sense.

Then the auction papers state that 'the jam factory is close to the Pixley Court Estate and is run in connection with it, forming a fine investment for anyone desiring a really first class farming estate'. The first point of relevance is that the factory is described as being close to the estate and not on it, or part of it. The second point is the mention that the factory is run in connection with the estate—that is, the estate grows the fruit and the factory processes it. It could be argued that Tom Davies wanted, ideally, to sell both sites and so to 'brand' the Ledbury factory with (arguably) its original name might emphasize the cohesiveness of the two auction lots and so persuade a potential buyer to take them both, rather than one or the other.

A further key point is that, in offering the Pixley Jam Factory, it is stated that the ground rent will be £45 per annum—exactly the figure agreed in 1921 between T E Davies Ltd and John Davies for the rent of the Fairtree Farm site for the Ledbury factory.

Finally, the auction papers give an excellent description of the factory which is up for sale. It is said to be:

> the most up-to-date bijou factory in the Midlands, being a single-storey factory standing in its own grounds of about three acres, close to station and docks for sugar, and in the centre of four of the best industrial centres. The factory comprises: large store, pulp

store, boiling room, filling room, packing room, engine house, meal room, offices, stationery stores etc with 25hp boiler, 25hp Tangye Steam Engine, eight large copper jam boilers, pulper, presser, peeler, stoning machines, petrol lorry.

This is no small scale operation or some back yard affair. It is a large business with expensive equipment and machinery and would require a considerable number of people to run it. It is almost inconceivable that something of this size would still be intact at Pixley Court in 1923, in parallel with a near identical factory at Ledbury that Tom Davies had started seven years earlier. It could be added that the above description ties in very well with descriptions of the Ledbury site given below and in the next chapter.

A very strong case can therefore be made for saying that, despite being called the 'Pixley Jam Factory', it was in fact the Ledbury Fairtree Farm site that Tom Davies unsuccessfully put up for sale in 1923.

There are, however, two counter points to all this which argue in favour of a factory at Pixley and one of them is particularly strong.

The first is that, in late 1916 when Tom Davies was defending his jam boiler from charges of absenteeism from the armed forces, he stated that he had 'a large contract to supply troops'. It could be asked whether, if he had only started his business that year, he would have had a large government contract quite so soon. That is a question which cannot now be answered.

The second, and much stronger, point is a single word in a single sentence in a single press cutting. In 1919, as noted earlier, Tom Davies was seeking to buy locally grown fruit for his factory. As part of this drive, a party of Herefordshire fruit growers visited the 'plantations of T E Davies at Pixley'. A report in the *Ledbury Guardian* says that there was a 'tour of the jam factory at Pixley'; it says that 'rhubarb and ginger was being prepared at the time [of the visit] and some four tons a day can be turned out with the work in full swing. All the girls wore white overalls and the place had an exceptionally clean and neat appearance'. It then added that the 'firm has other factories at Worthington and Ledbury'. The word other clearly implies that there were, indeed, two separate factories, one at Ledbury and one at Pixley.

If one wanted to make a case against a Pixley operation, it would be possible to argue this was an error in a press report; they referred to a factory at Worthington when presumably Withington was meant; so perhaps the writer was not a local man and confused something that was said during the visit and the word 'other' should never have been included. It is even

THE GOOD OLD DAYS

It is now a near-impossibility to know what it was like working in the jam factory in the 1920s. However, long service by staff was the norm in those days. Ada Phillips began working at the jam factory in 1927 when Tom Davies was still in charge. She was still there in 1974 and at that time recalled some aspects of life half a century earlier.

Fruit bottling was an important line —she remembered rhubarb, damsons, blackberries and plums in particular, as these had a special pattern for packing into square jars; snap tops had to be fitted before the jars were heated in big round pans.

Lemon curd making was a rather different operation, partly due to the use of granulated sugar. Each open copper pan had its own operator and the contents had to be stirred the whole time until ready—fine on a cold day in winter, but on a hot July day, it was a different story.

Mrs Phillips particularly remembered the apple jam which was made from apple pulp. It was delicious—'not just jelly, but real jam' and it was generally filled into 28lb tins or barrels.

Each barrel had a tap, so these were the forerunners of the 15cwt tanks to be introduced very much later in the factory's life. The apples and also plums had originally been cooked in vats, filled into barrels and with sulphur dioxide added. The barrels were then rolled away and stacked on their sides, three high, on railway sleepers, until the fruit was required for jam boiling.

One or two pound glass jars arrived in bales of straw. These had to be unpacked, and the jars washed—by hand of course.

possible that the tour went across Tom Davies's estates and ended up at the Ledbury factory but the writer just assumed that the factory they were seeing was at Pixley.

Again, the 1918 press report quoted earlier about a surfeit of blackberries referred to fruit arriving at Ledbury Station; if fruit was being delivered to Pixley Court, then Ashperton would have been the more natural and normal station for this. Equally, when Tom Davies advertised in 1918 for fruit to purchase, he said this could be received at Ledbury or Withington; there is no mention of Pixley.

The evidence is difficult to interpret. However, it is hard to accept that, if Tom Davies started a factory from scratch at Fairtree Farm in 1916 (as he most certainly did), then any operation at Pixley Court would, in 1923, have been described as 'the most up-to-date bijou factory in the Midlands'. The other aspects of the sale—for example, use of the words 'close to' but not 'on' Pixley Court—only serve to reinforce our view that the proposed 1923 sale was of the Ledbury site, and not one at Pixley. This view is supported by one of John Davies's granddaughters who lived at Pixley Court as a child in the 1920s; she is adamant that there was never any jam factory there (although this would not preclude the possibility of any pre-1920 operation).

It is hard to conceive that there were large scale jam making operations at both Pixley and Ledbury, owned by the same man and running at the same time for any significant period. However, this would not rule out the possibility that there might have been a much smaller scale operation at Pixley, possibly for just using the surplus fruit from the estate itself. So the tantalising possibility remains that it was here at pre-1920s, and very probably pre-war Pixley, that Tom Davies learnt the art of jam making which he was later to use on a much larger scale at both Withington and Ledbury.

2 ⤜ Rescue and Recovery

Ledbury Preserves (1928) Ltd

The ins and outs of late 1927 and the first half of 1928 remain somewhat misty. A few skeleton facts are known but certain names—especially of companies—seem to repeat themselves in a way that rules out coincidence, but which does not supply a logical answer. These facts will have to be strung together with a degree of imagination and supposition to try and make a cohesive story. In short, the known facts are that:

• The Midland Bank (which held a £6,000 debenture on Ledbury Preserves) put in a receiver in late 1927.

• In December 1927 an Accountant, Albert Callan from accountancy firm Baker Sutton & Co, arrived to look at the company's books.

• At that time, one of the directors of Ledbury Preserves was a gentleman named Watkin Jones. Watkin Jones was also an executive director of a South Wales provision and bakery concern called D Jones Dickinson. This is of considerable relevance given that D Jones Dickinson was shortly to acquire Ledbury Preserves.

• In February 1928, D Jones Dickinson considered buying out Ledbury Preserves but at that point decided not to pursue the purchase. Within a few months, they had changed their minds and acquired the jam factory, rebranding it as Ledbury Preserves (1928) Ltd.

• The then Chairman of D Jones Dickinson was a partner in Baker Sutton & Co.

• Albert Callan was to stay on at Ledbury Preserves as its general manager and to become a director. Much later he was also to become a director of D Jones Dickinson.

• Another director of Ledbury Preserves (1928) Ltd was, as with D Jones Dickinson, to be a partner from Baker Sutton & Co.

It is worth retracing these steps and trying to join the facts together with a degree of (hopefully) inspired guesswork. However, this triangular relationship between Ledbury Preserves, D Jones Dickinson and Baker Sutton is intriguing and may never be fully explained.

The financial situation of the old Ledbury Preserves looked pretty dire as 1927 came to an end and their bankers called in a receiver. Receivership does not mean the company is actually bankrupt but arises when a creditor who is owed money by a company puts in someone to see if there is a way of recovering that debt. A receiver is someone, generally an accountant, sent into the company to take control of any assets on which the creditor (in this case, the bank) has a call.

Since the creditor, ie the Midland Bank, is the one who calls in the receiver, it would be reasonable to assume that, in this case, the bank asked the firm of accountants Baker Sutton & Co to look into the position of Ledbury Preserves. Baker Sutton was a significant concern, based in Eldon Street in the City of London and which had offices in New York as well. Much later they were to be integrated into the bigger company of Ernst & Whinney and so later still became part of the current Ernst & Young.

However, it cannot have been a coincidence that Baker Sutton was selected to be the receiver when that partnership was already auditor and had appointed two nominees as directors of D Jones Dickinson, the company that was to buy out Ledbury Preserves. (The ability of one concern to be both auditor and director was not illegal under company law at this stage.) It is possible that, when the subject of receivership was broached by the bank, the man who was already a director of both companies—Watkin Jones—suggested the name of Baker Sutton to the bank.

There is nothing untoward in Watkin Jones being a director of Ledbury Preserves. We saw in the previous chapter that, during the mid 1920s, Ledbury Preserves acquired a number of external directors, most of whom were from South Wales grocery companies. While it is not known when he joined the board of Ledbury Preserves, Watkin Jones might well have been 'recruited' in this way. What is more remarkable is that nothing has been found in the minute books of D Jones Dickinson which mentions this pre-buy-out relationship. When such a representation was agreed, it would appear to have been off the record.

So, however it came about, Baker Sutton & Co was appointed receiver. The partner in charge of this investigation was J Jeffery Baker and in December 1927, he sent a young accountant, Albert Callan, then in his late 20s, from London to Ledbury to go through the books. The Callan family has always understood that Albert Callan was sent there 'to close the place down' but that he found 'it might be saved if it had a sufficient injection of new funds'.

But where was this capital injection to come from?

The ultimate answer to that question was to be 'from D Jones Dickinson'.

That company had been founded in 1895 and was both a provisions mer-
chant, with depots at Cardiff and Swansea, and a cake manufacturer with a
factory at Dowlais on the outskirts of Merthyr Tydfil. With its head office
in Cardiff, the geographical distance between it and Ledbury Preserves was
not large, while there was clearly a complementary synergy between their
businesses.

At that time though, the Welsh company had some other significant
issues on its plate. On one Sunday evening in July 1927, there had been a
major fire at its Dowlais factory which led to the total cessation of business
there. An insurance claim was in hand and this would eventually be set-
tled for almost £9,000, but with D Jones Dickinson responsible for carrying
out the rebuilding and renovation work. In addition, it had just weathered
the General Strike of 1926 and—while obviously unknown to them at that
time—the Great Depression of 1929 and later was just around the corner.

No doubt there were behind-the-scenes discussions of which nothing
is now known. Watkin Jones would have discussed the position with his
colleagues in South Wales, while Jeffery Baker would have shared thoughts
with Harry Keasley, his fellow partner at Baker Sutton and board chairman
of D Jones Dickinson.

As far as firm evidence goes, the first recorded discussion of a possible
takeover took place on 10 February 1928 at a routine meeting of the D Jones
Dickinson board. No decision was reached but they agreed to visit the Ledbury site for themselves later that month. They obviously appreciated the
need for speed—or possibly secrecy—since it was just nine days later, and
on a Sunday, that they came to Ledbury for the first time. The minutes of
their meeting held that same day in Ledbury state:

> 'The Board, having had a full opportunity of examining the jam
> factory at Ledbury and the position generally in regard thereto,
> came to the conclusion that for the present no advantage could be
> gained by making an offer for the works as it was felt that only an
> offer at a low value could be made. It was therefore resolved to do
> nothing further in the matter for the time being.'

Within three months though, that position had changed. On 2 May 1928,
the directors of D Jones Dickinson again met at Ledbury 'in order to dis-
cuss the maximum offer they could make for the stock, goodwill and lease
of the works at Ledbury'. After negotiations with the directors of Ledbury
Preserves—who may have felt that in reality they had little choice in the

matter—they offered £1,500 for the lease and goodwill and a further £1,150 for stock in trade. This latter offer was contingent on the new owners being able to retain the name of Ledbury Preserves Ltd. There was nothing sentimental about this, nor was it a case of paying more for the goodwill of the business; it was simply that the existing stock of bottles and labels could continue to be used by the new company!

The new company, 'Ledbury Preserves (1928) Ltd', was formally incorporated on 21 July 1928 with a paid-up share capital of £10,000, the whole of the shares being in the name of the company (ie D Jones Dickinson) or its nominees. Two directors were appointed—Jeffery Baker and Watkin Jones. Albert Callan was to stay on to run the company and almost certainly reporting to, and under the watchful eye of, the very hands-on Watkin Jones.

The old Ledbury Preserves had to be formally wound up and so continued a legal existence for another two years until a final winding-up meeting was held on 14 May 1930.

A Flight of Fancy

As remarked earlier, the three-way relationship at this time between Ledbury Preserves, D Jones Dickinson and Baker Sutton remains intriguing. The story as given above contains quite a few coincidences that cannot be fully explained. Perhaps there was another, hidden, agenda behind all this. While it must be stressed that what follows is supposition with little evidence to support it, it has to be admitted that it might be an alternative version of the story.

In late 1927, when Tom Davies had sold his preference shares in Ledbury Preserves, a condition agreed with the company had been that the other directors should raise £3,000 in cash to help put the company back on its feet. This had not materialised. Watkin Jones would have been one of these other directors and one would have expected him to take this back to the board of the other company where he was a director, D Jones Dickinson—yet nothing to that effect appears in their board minutes of the time.

So no one advanced any cash to Ledbury Preserves, not even D Jones Dickinson, despite the fact that at that time they would have been cash rich, with almost £9,000 in hand from the insurance claim following the disastrous fire earlier that year at their Dowlais factory. Perhaps D Jones Dickinson decided that they had no wish to prop up an ailing company for the benefit of others as well as themselves, but saw a potential opportunity to acquire Ledbury Preserves as their own subsidiary.

The financial difficulties at Ledbury Preserves were such that their bankers decided to call in the receivers. In such a situation, it is normal to assume that it was the bank which took the initiative but it is not impossible to imagine the directors of D Jones Dickinson making the first move and alerting the bank to the potential problems that existed at the jam factory. In doing so—and remembering that Baker Sutton were providing the board chairman and auditors for D Jones Dickinson—they might well have suggested that Baker Sutton would be willing to act as receivers should the bank wish to investigate the position further. The bank, of course, did wish to investigate and so the receivers were brought in.

Baker Sutton then confirmed that Ledbury Preserves did have difficulties but could survive with an appropriate injection of capital—but where from? Watkin Jones suggested that D Jones Dickinson might be interested and the directors from that company make a visit to Ledbury—quietly and on a Sunday. They formally told Ledbury Preserves that, since 'only an offer at a low value could be made', they would not be pursuing the matter further.

No doubt the other directors of Ledbury Preserves were concerned at this. They could see the company going into liquidation and such shares as they held becoming totally worthless. Perhaps they subsequently asked D Jones Dickinson what 'an offer at low value' actually meant and a figure, as explained above, totalling £2,650 was agreed. The other directors of Ledbury Preserves breathed a sigh of relief and gracefully backed out of the story and a new and highly significant phase in the life of Ledbury Preserves began.

Regeneration

Albert Callan was to prove a very suitable and capable general manager for Ledbury Preserves, keeping the company on the financial straight and narrow, but he could not do everything single-handedly and certainly would not have had the knowledge or experience to run the actual jam making operation of the factory. So enter Llewellyn Jones, brother of Watkin Jones, as works manager. Despite apparently having a background more in farming than in manufacturing, 'Old Man Jones' (as he was affectionately known to staff) was to run the factory itself efficiently and effectively for the next 16 years until his death in 1944. Both Albert Callan and Llewellyn Jones were to be appointed directors of Ledbury Preserves by the early 1930s.

All this may smack of a cosy nepotism, but it would not have been unusual for the time. The need to ensure that directors of a company could not also be its auditors was very soon to be addressed and the Companies Act, which was implemented in 1929, made this an essential split.

These appointments at Ledbury Preserves (1928) Ltd meant that some people had to move house! Albert Callan had been born and raised in London but now moved to live in Malvern, bringing his parents with him to live nearby. Llewellyn Jones had owned a farm in Chepstow but now had to up sticks and move initially to Cradley, but later to a bungalow called 'Overseas', which still stands and is just a few hundred yards up the road from the jam factory.

Staff of the Finishing Room and Despatch Bay in the 1930s. Back row: Bill Walters, Arch Barnet, Bert Jenkins Front row: Gillie Perrel, Vic Player

Another key appointment at this time was to be Bill Walters. He joined the company in 1931 and was to remain there until his retirement in 1969. It was here he was to meet his wife-to-be, Cicely (Cis) whom he married in 1934. The jam factory was Bill's life; he arrived there every day at 6am and it is said that he never took any holidays. On retiring, he was owed so much holiday pay that the factory continued to send wages to him for a full year! He was to become Transport Manager and ran a tight ship. If any lorries were delayed, the drivers had to call on Bill at home to account for their lateness. This 'finger on the pulse' was not just a 1930s or 1940s thing. Staff in the 1960s say that Bill knew exactly where every driver was at any moment. If you needed to contact someone urgently, you could ask Bill who would look at his watch and say something on the lines of: 'he'll just be going over Shap Fell now—he'll be at the Cosy Café in 10 minutes, so try ringing him there.' And he was always right!

Water was essential to the operation of the factory and although they were on the mains, an emergency back-up supply was thought a good idea. There was a well in the factory grounds (by the tall chimney at the far end of the site) but this was not a natural source of water and had to be kept topped-up. On two days each week, and up to four times on each of those days, lorries were sent to a natural well near Bromsberrow where water was pumped into tanks on the back of the lorries and taken back to the factory.

With new owners and fresh capital, this was a time of regeneration for Ledbury Preserves. Business grew, not least by supplying 'industrial jam'—that is, jam used in the making of cakes, biscuits and the like, rather than jam in jars as an end-product in itself—to customers, most probably including their new parent company for use in their confectionery.

Various financial agreements were made between D Jones Dickinson and its new subsidiary company in Ledbury. Basically, the parent company advanced various monies to the jam factory, which in turn had to repay agreed sums annually, as well as producing a profit, with share dividends from this obviously also going back to their Welsh owners. In addition to the initial capital injection, a further substantial bank loan was arranged and guaranteed by the parent in 1936 for additional buildings at Ledbury to enable the jam factory to 'maintain and increase its business'. By way of example, the annual sum being repaid was £4,000 in the mid 1930s, but this increased to £10,000 by the end of the decade.

Factory Girls in the early 1930s. On the left, Hilary Gordon; on the right, Cis Walters

A new French barn was built at Ledbury for storage in 1929, a new syrup plant was added in 1933 and a further factory room in 1936. There was a new garage in 1938 and a boilerhouse in 1939. Some things came down though and not necessarily as part of a plan. In 1936, there was a severe gale and an 80 foot high metal chimney stack collapsed somewhat faster than it had been put up.

It was also in the mid 1930s when, according to company tradition, the company started supplying products to Marks & Spencer. While the exact year that this began is not known, Marks & Spencer's own archives confirm that Ledbury Preserves was providing jam for their stores by 1939, something discussed further in Chapter 8.

It is also true that by the early 1930s Ledbury Preserves was making a profit for its parent company—and this was a much needed profit. By the time of their AGM at the end of 1929, the directors of D Jones Dickinson were referring to the 'depression existing in South Wales which had adversely affected the company's trading'. The following year, they could not afford to pay a final dividend without drawing on reserves, which they declined to do. While a small dividend was paid in 1931, this was not to be repeated in either 1932 or 1933 when the company suffered an overall trading loss.

By 1935, the chairman of D Jones Dickinson at their AGM—and this was still Harry Kearsley of Baker Sutton & Co—said that the profits of the subsidiary company (ie Ledbury Preserves) were 'showing a very satisfactory return', although trading conditions remained difficult for the parent itself, a position to continue for some years to come. For example, in 1938 there had been 'satisfactory profits' at the subsidiary company but losses at their Cardiff and Dowlais branches. He referred to attempts to get rid of the Dowlais plant—they were unsuccessful in this—while mentioning the fact that 'the depopulation in South Wales and the hope of an improvement in trade resulting from the government's scheme in the distressed areas had not resulted in an increase of labour'.

It may well be that their 1928 purchase of Ledbury Preserves had prevented D Jones Dickinson from sinking entirely.

Happier Days

New buildings, industrial jam, the Welsh depression and Marks & Spencer notwithstanding, a date that would have remained in the memory of many staff was Thursday 30 April 1931, for that is when they all enjoyed an extra day's holiday. This was to mark the wedding of their General Manager, Albert Callan. His bride was also well-known at the factory. Llewellyn Jones, the Works Manager, had two daughters—Dorothy and Ethel—both of whom worked at Ledbury Preserves and it was Dorothy who had caught the eye of Callan. At the time of the wedding, he was 30 and she was 21.

The marriage took place at Christ Church in Malvern, and all the staff—nearly 50 in number—went to the ceremony, 'the women [travelling] in a char-a-banc and the men by the works lorry'. After the ceremony, the newly-weds—'escorted by the work-people'—returned to the jam works at Ledbury where a party was held in the works canteen to which all the staff were invited. At the end of the party, the newly-weds were given 'a boisterous send-off' by the assembled guests, accompanied by blasts on the works hooter. The hooter, used to signal the start and end of the day's shifts, could be heard over most of the town and was a well-known (if not, perhaps, always well-loved) sound in Ledbury. Having said that, it was noted for its accuracy and a good number of townspeople would both then and in later years, unthinkingly, check their watches whenever they heard the hooter. No doubt they were left suitably confused on that April afternoon in 1931.

Staff outings were also to become a regular feature of factory life. There were annual charabanc trips, certainly from the early 1930s onwards to places that staff in those days would probably otherwise never have seen. Although full details of these outings have not survived, it is known by way of example that the 1933 trip was to Portsmouth.

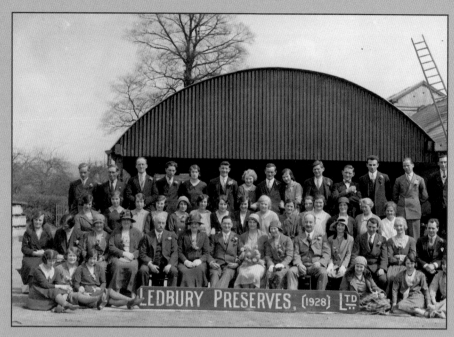

30 April 1931—the wedding reception of Albert Callan and Dorothy Jones who are in the centre of the picture. Llewellyn Jones is immediately above the '1928' wording.

CHILDHOOD MEMORIES

Albert and Dorothy Callan had two sons, and in the late 1930s and early 1940s, Albert would, from time to time, take one or other of his sons with him to the jam factory. They would go there in the family car—a Standard 8—from their home in Malvern, over the hills and down through Chances Pitch to Ledbury. This was not on the 'new' smooth road from British Camp downwards, but on the old road that ended in a very steep and dangerous T junction at the top of Chances Pitch where you joined the 'main' road running from Colwall to Ledbury. The junction was 'hell in winter' when covered in snow. In Ledbury itself, it was straight ahead at Top Cross into New Street, and then branch right into Little Marcle Road, passing the gasworks and on to the jam factory.

Once there, and in the days before health and safety was an issue, the elder son, Brian, remembers being given the run of the place. In the main building, he recalls there was steam everywhere and the overwhelming smell of the jam being boiled in the vats. These were about four feet high, and four feet in diameter, but seemed massive to a youthful nine year old. The women stirring the jam loved to see him there and would make a great fuss of him.

Near to the vats was an auxiliary engine room. To a young boy, this was a fantastic place. It held a gas oil engine with a towering six foot flywheel; painted green, it looked absolutely immaculate and in pristine condition—today it would take pride of place in any industrial museum! The main boilerhouse was across a narrow internal road from the factory and this held two or three coal fired boilers to provide the steam to boil the jam and also a small steam engine to provide the drive for any rotary action required in the factory such as rotating tables.

Next to the boilerhouse was the cooper's area; barrels were needed to store partly processed or preserved fruit so that there would still be plenty available outside the harvesting season to make jam. All the barrels needed by the factory were made on site and it was fascinating to watch the hot metal hoops being hammered down over the staves of the barrels.

In the middle of the factory was the Works Manager's office—a glass-sided room from where his grandfather, Llewellyn Jones, could see all that was going on. At the opposite end of the factory to the boilerhouse was the loading bay and here, Brian could 'help' in loading the lorries with boxes filled with jars of jam, although as he readily admits, no doubt actually getting in the way!

Staff leaving the Ledbury Market House for a chara-banc outing in the early 30s. There are two gentlemen roughly in the centre of the picture; the one on the left is works manager Llewellyn Jones.

3 ⁓ The War and After

Wartime Difficulties

In the light of the widespread suffering and the terrible toll of human lives brought about by the Second World War, it may seem petty to talk of the business and economic circumstances faced by one small factory in a rural English town. Nonetheless, they are an integral aspect of the story of the Ledbury jam factory, although no doubt the problems they faced were typical of those experienced by many other similar businesses across the country.

The outbreak of war does not seem to have had any immediate or drastic effect on the company. Indeed, at the December 1939 AGM of the parent company, D Jones Dickinson, there was not even any mention of the hostilities. It was simply recorded that the profits at Ledbury Preserves 'had been more than maintained' while the losses at their other branches, largely caused by the severe 1930s depression in South Wales, had been reduced.

It was at this period that 'war jam' as it was known took on a new significance. Tom Davies had claimed back in 1916 that he had 'a large contract to supply troops' and it is possible that this contract had continued ever since, but certainly the importance of this jam grew during the Second World War. Produced by Ledbury Preserves for the Ministry of War, 'war jam' came in two unusual sizes: the larger was in 2lb tins, largely destined for NAAFI canteens and other military catering units, while the smaller—in 9oz tins, and containing a built-in tin opener to get at it!—was part of the emergency rations for the troops. The latter size needed special dispensation since, at that time, all jam had to be packaged in standard size jars—usually 1lb, and certainly not the oddity of 9oz. The production of war jam was to continue well beyond the end of the war and was still a key line well into the 1950s.

Supplies were problematic; jam was on ration, while sugar was in short supply and its distribution controlled by the government. Tin for containers and glass for jars was not always easy to obtain, but in the main, sufficient supplies came through to keep the production lines going.

It was remarkably easy to fall foul of all the various government restrictions and controls. In 1944, the parent company D Jones Dickinson was prosecuted for the use of 'edible oil other than by permit'. The company had believed that, at time of purchase, the oil was off ration, but they were still found guilty of a technical offence and had to pay a small fine.

Petrol was restricted and this meant difficulties, both for the distribution network and the sales staff. Attempts were made by the parent company, especially in the immediate post-war years, to obtain an increase in the petrol allowance for the salesmen in the hopes of building up the business again.

Daytime production at the factory meant that many delivery runs were made at night and this was a hazardous task. The lights of the lorries were shuttered, with just a rectangular slot left clear and very little light emerging. The dangers this presented were of particular concern to the works manager, Llewellyn Jones, his deputy Geoff Knight and to Bill Walters.

The overnight journeys were usually to London, taking preserves both for the forces—the 'war jam'—and for more general distribution. The drivers would sleep during the day at a London distribution depot while their products were taken to various drop-off points by local men.

They would then return to Ledbury the following night, bring with them either sugar or glass (for jars), often collected from the Silvertown area in London's Docklands or from Brentford. (After the war, the distribution depot used was run by Arthur Sturge, a former employee of Ledbury Preserves.)

Sugar also came to Ledbury by rail and having arrived, it had to be stored somewhere; issues of both capacity and security meant that locations in addition to the factory itself were needed. Places used included the dance hall at the Royal Oak pub in Ledbury's Southend and in the Sunday School room of the Congregational Chapel in Church Lane (where the Butcher's Row Musuem now stands). From there, it had to be taken on a sacktruck, rattling over the cobbles down Church Lane to a waiting lorry to take it down to the jam factory.

Staffing was also a problem. Conscription took workers, both from the factory itself and from the farms that supplied the fruit. Land Army Girls worked hard in Herefordshire to help cover the shortage of agricultural workers. Since the factory had a high percentage of older women on its workforce, the situation was not as serious as in some other industries.

It is not known how Ledbury Preserves treated those of its staff who were called up, but it seems very likely that they would have followed the pattern set by their parent company. In 1942, D Jones Dickinson considered 'the question of allowances to men and women in the services'; after some discussion, it was agreed that any of the pre-war staff who joined up should be given an allowance of £1 a week for men and 10 shillings (ie 50p) for women.

Staff were also involved with the Home Guard, Bill Walters being among the first to volunteer on the outbreak of war. They had to provide their own guns and were trained at Kilbury Camp, a good point from which to guard access to Ledbury from the east. On a more mundane level, it was also close to Frith Wood which was good for rabbiting—a necessary addition to the meat ration!

Later, in the early 1940s, all Ledbury Preserves men had to train as Air Raid Wardens, mainly to do nightwatch on the factory roof. When a bomb fell nearby in Falcon Lane, Lord Haw Haw was to claim it had fallen on the jam factory itself—an interesting bit of propaganda which perhaps casts an insight into the importance of the factory to national supplies.

Although the business profits of Ledbury Preserves were steadily increasing, this did not filter through to the accounts of the group. The government, more and more in need of additional income as the war went on, introduced an Excess Profits Tax which strictly limited what could be retained. As noted at the 1944 D Jones Dickinson AGM: 'Although Ledbury Preserves showed an increased trading profit, this was absorbed by taxation and this will naturally be the result in future years while the Excess Profits Tax remains at 100%'. It was not until after the war that the tax was rescinded, and certain excess monies received by the government were returned to companies, this resulting in a one-off windfall for Ledbury Preserves in 1946 of just over £19,000.

Sidelines

Ledbury Preserves was a keen participant in raising money during the war years for the 'Red Cross Agriculture Fund'. When the war started in 1939, the British Red Cross and St John Ambulance had many calls for help on the Home Front, ranging from welfare work, caring for injured servicemen and other training and support roles, but money was needed to do all this. Traditionally, they had raised funds from the wealthier sections of society but at this time they decided to appeal to wage earners and particular sections of the community—not an easy task when paper rationing limited the number of posters and leaflets that could be produced. However, by the end of the war a total of £54 million had been raised, an incredible sum by any standards.

One of the specific ways of raising money was through the 'Agriculture Fund'—an appeal to that particular section of the community. The Appeal's Committee raised money in seven main ways—for example from shows and exhibitions or auctions of livestock and produce—but the way in which Ledbury became involved was through a concentrated series of social events.

In the last two months of 1942, for example, a total of sixteen parties and dances were held in Ledbury and the surrounding villages. A total of over 2,000 people turned up and a profit of several hundred pounds was raised for the fund. The parties were close to the heart of works manager Llewellyn Jones, were hosted by his deputy Geoff Knight, and had been organised by the Entertainments Committee of Ledbury Preserves who had 'worked day and night including Sundays to keep the programme at full pitch'. These obviously well supported events ended that year with a massive festive season dance at Ledbury's Drill Hall—now the site of the Somerfield supermarket.

A similar programme was held each year from 1940-43 (and again in 1945) and included dance evenings, Christmas parties, talent events and whist drives. It was noted at one of these events that there had been no refreshments provided. Geoff Knight explained that 'he felt that in such times as those through which the country was passing, the company would not mind foregoing refreshments.'

On a somewhat more unusual note, Ledbury Preserves was taken to court in October 1943 on the grounds that they had supplied a quantity of raspberry jam 'which did not conform to the Jam and Marmalade Maximum Prices Order through being deficient of the necessary percentage of raspberries'. (Raspberries, incidentally, came mainly from Scotland despite the transport problems of the time.) The case was heard at the Gloucester City Police Court and it was argued by the public analyst to Gloucestershire that the fruit in the sample did not exceed fifteen per cent, while the order required a minimum of twenty per cent. Ledbury Preserves called in another analyst from a trade association who disputed the findings of the first analyst! The magistrates found for Ledbury Preserves and ordered the prosecution to contribute twenty guineas towards the cost of the defence.

Changes at the Top

In late May 1943, Albert Callan, the General Manager of Ledbury Preserves, took a well-earned break from his work at the factory. He and his wife Dorothy went for a few days to Bournemouth. He was never to return to Ledbury.

Albert Callan

They were due to come home from Bournemouth on Saturday 22 May but at the last minute, decided to stay on for a few more days. A daylight raid by German aircraft took place on the town on Tuesday 25 May and the hotel where they were staying was hit by a bomb. Both Albert and Dorothy Callan were killed.

Just 15 months earlier Albert Callan had been appointed a director of D Jones Dickinson, as well as being a director of Ledbury Preserves, and DJD Chairman Harry Keasley said at their AGM:

'In the first place I should like to allude to the loss which we sustained earlier in the year by the death of Mr Callan through enemy action while on a short vacation. He was appointed a director of this company last year and from its inception in 1928, he was manager of your subsidiary company and ably assisted in building up that business. His loss has been a sad blow to his co-directors and staff.'

There seems little doubt that without Albert Callan's initial insight and subsequent leadership, Ledbury Preserves (1928) Ltd would never have been formed, and consequently there would have been no jam factory in Ledbury for the following 80 years.

His funeral took place at Malvern Wells Cemetery but only a small proportion of the large number of those attending could get into the small cemetery church; over 100 employees of Ledbury Preserves lined the pathway to the grave.

A further tragedy was to strike both the company and the family a year later when, in June 1944, Callan's father-in-law and the factory's works manager, Llewellyn Jones was to die. This was not war-related, however. At the age of 67, he was taken ill but continued to come to work until a fortnight before his death. It was noted that:

'The news of his death caused deep regret among the 150 employees of the company, by whom he was held in the highest esteem on account of his keen interest in their welfare. He took little part in public life, devoting his whole life to the business, but he took considerable interest in Ledbury Cottage Hospital and inaugurated an agreed contributory scheme among all his employees which has proved a great help to the hospital finances.

He had also given generously to the Red Cross Agriculture Fund.'

With two of the leading lights of Ledbury Preserves dying within a year of each other, it is natural to ask: 'Who took over?' Regrettably, the answer is far from clear.

There were three key players at the factory at this time:
• Walter Hodges who had joined the company around 1937/38 and who was responsible for sales.
• Ken Baker, brother of Jeffery Baker who had been invalided out of the forces, and who now looked after the company accounts; and
• Geoff Knight who, on the death of Llewellyn Jones, became works manager and had responsibility not just for the factory production lines, but also for transport and fruit buying.

However, it is far from clear who, if anyone of this triumvirate, was in overall charge. While some staff of the time talk of Walter Hodges as being managing director, this did not happen until well into the 1950s; others have referred to 'Mr Baker being in charge' but cannot be sure if this was Ken Baker or his brother Jeffery Baker, a non-executive director. Others have said they were not aware of any one of the above three being in overall charge, while others have referred to 'people coming up from Cardiff', a likely reference to Watkin Jones.

On balance, it seems likely that each of the three executives mentioned above (Walter Hodges, Ken Baker and Geoff Knight) had clearly defined areas of responsibility and that any overall direction and strategy was provided by Jeffery Baker and the very hands-on Watkin Jones.

From this position, in the post-war period, Walter Hodges was to emerge to become the man at the top; he was to become a director of Ledbury Preserves in, it is believed, 1948 and was then formally appointed general manager sometime in the 1950s.

The Wartime Factory

Mrs Nancy Maddox began work at Ledbury Preserves in 1936; she left for a time in 1945, before rejoining in 1948. Mrs Margery Probert started at the factory when she left school in 1942 and—apart from one year off in 1948—was still there in 1974. Both ladies well remember how jam was made in those days—very hard work when compared with the modern process, but like other people who took part in it, they agree they enjoyed it all.

The hours were 8 am until 6 pm on Monday to Friday and from 8am to 12 noon on Saturday, although during the fresh fruit season, working through to 8pm or 9pm was quite usual. The normal weekly wage for the ladies was 25 shillings (£1.25) before the war. All the jam was boiled in open pans of course. When it was ready, the pan would be lifted by two ladies up to the cooler.

From the left: Dora Kale, Nancy Maddox and Josie Bevan in 1949

Empty jars were put ready on a round table that for ever turned, and the filler had a jug, filled from the cooler with a scoop. He or she filled each jar as it came round and what an effect that had on one's hands and little finger by the end of the day! Every jar was then wiped and a waxed disc placed on the hot jam—but no cap at this point. The jars were placed in a crate which held 20 on one layer, with 12 layers of hot jam jars all uncapped. The crate was wheeled away to join others until they were stacked 12 high, to cool down; a day or two later they would all be fetched back to the finishing room.

Here the waxed discs were removed, new ones put in, and in the case of the 1lb or 2lb jars, the tops which were then fitted were made of tin or cardboard. Next, the jars went to the labelling room, where the glue was put on the labels with a paste brush and the label put on the jar. The record speed for one day was 21 gross; orders were timed at 14 gross which had to be achieved each day. Finally, the jars were inspected, packed into wooden boxes and taken into the loading bay.

Table jam was also filled into 7lb stone jars and these were difficult to stack; no two were exactly the same, so that they could not be made level when stacking. Inevitably there would be spilling from time to time.

Confectionery jam had its own problems. After cooking in the open pans, it was poured into big bins which, in themselves, were heavier than their contents. These were lifted onto long coolers, emptied and the jam persuaded to cool by being stirred with rubber scrapers. Then the jam was

emptied into another pan with a tap and filled out into 28 lb tins. The jam was covered with a tissue, the tins stacked on a truck, taken to a cooling area and stacked five tins high. On one occasion, a whole battalion of tins of jam had been newly stacked, and someone caught the edge of the front row with a little hand truck. Over went the whole row, which pushed the next row, and the next , on and on, until all the tins were overturned and the jam deep on the floor.

Mrs Doris Cessario began working at the factory on 3 February 1941. She well remembers the processes already described. One extra point noted was that during the war, the apple jam was filled into 28lb tins; these were then despatched for the making of toffee apples. During the evening shift, displaced persons (from abroad) continued filling out the apple jam and other products.

Everything in the factory was done by hand. The women there wore heavy duty rubber aprons and rubber gloves, as well as a hairnet and wooden clogs to protect their feet from over-spills of boiling hot jam. However careful people were, occasional mistakes were inevitable and the sound of a sharp cry could be heard as jam splashed and someone scalded themselves.

Post-war Times

The war was barely over before the board of D Jones Dickinson was to receive an approach from another company which was potentially inter-ested in acquiring Ledbury Preserves. It was in July 1945 that the St Martin

Preserving Company, under the leadership of one Colonel Willie Tickler, asked the board if they would be interested in 'some form of amalgamation' of the two businesses. This, however, was polite-speak for a takeover. Jeffery Baker called on Colonel Tickler to see what they had in mind—and what they had in mind was an acquisition of Ledbury Preserves, the purchase to be made by an issue of shares by the purchasing company.

This proposal did not suit the D Jones Dickinson board at all. With the war ending, and still with memories of the pre-war recession, they were anxious to expand their business outside the South Wales area and Ledbury Preserves might have provided one route for doing this. In addition, they could see little purpose in exchanging their holding in a wholly owned subsidiary for a minority holding in a public company.

On these grounds, the board were unanimous in rejecting the proposed takeover but did feel it was worthwhile meeting again with Colonel Tickler to see whether any manufacturing or sales agreement might be arranged which would be to their joint advantages. This route obviously did not suit Tickler, since no response was received from him.

On the outskirts of the town is the Ledbury Preserves (1928) Ltd. factory, which at the peak summer period employs 450 people. Throughout the year 6,000 tons of jams are produced. Filling tins are Miss Barbara Morris, of 74, Bridge Street, Ledbury (left) and Mrs. F. K. Richardson, of 175, Homend Street, Ledbury.

8 February 1953

Just how anxious the board members were to expand their business is perhaps open to a little scepticism. They were approached in 1946 by Marks & Spencer to see if they could supply cakes and puddings for their stores. What would appear to have been a golden opportunity to take their fortunes forward was greeted with some degree of coolness. The company did provide samples to M&S who were satisfied with the product, but the D Jones Dickinson Board resolved that they 'should undertake this work [only if] it did not interfere with local trade'.

D Jones Dickinson received another approach in these post-war years, but of a very different kind. With the Labour Party winning a landslide victory in the General Election, they were contacted in 1947 by a Rear Admiral Figgins who suggested that the company should make a subscription to the Conservative and Unionist Central Office 'for the purpose of fighting socialism and communism and, incidentally, the nationalisation of industry'. This proposal was declined.

Trading by the jam factory was encouraging. Although 1947 had started with a harsh winter, the summer was good and there was a bumper fruit harvest. Ledbury Preserves decided to take full advantage of this and arranged increased overdraft facilities with their bankers in order to lay in additional stocks of fruit. This was to serve them well with increased trading and increased profits in the year to come. Jam came 'off ration' in 1949, although sugar remained a government-controlled commodity. It was also a time of new facilities for Ledbury Preserves, with the boiler house being extended in 1949, while the following year saw a totally new boiler installed.

Staff and Staffing

There are no records of how the staff of Ledbury Preserves marked the end of the war, but it is likely that they followed the example of their parent company; if so, a 'Victory Outing' was arranged, with the company paying for the hire of coaches, and providing a free breakfast. If this did happen in Ledbury, it would have continued the idea of 'char-a-banc outings' which had started in the 1930s and which were to become an annual event in the late 1940s. In the days before the private car, motorways or long annual holidays, these expeditions were a highlight of the year. They worked like this.

Each year—usually in September or October when the fruit harvest was over and the high level of seasonal work completed—the company paid for a coach trip to some seaside resort—places could be quite far afield for the times, and included Blackpool, Weston, Rhyl and Southsea. Staff would leave Ledbury early on a Saturday morning and reach their destination in time for lunch. The afternoon was free time, often spent playing bowls on the green if the weather permitted, and there would then be a theatre visit in the evening. The journey home was through the night, arriving in Ledbury around 5 or 6 am on the Sunday morning. It has been commented that the Monday after this 'was usually a rather quiet day'.

A voluntary scheme was also set up to help staff save for Christmas. Under the name of the 'Fairtree Savings Scheme', an agreed sum was stopped from the employee's wages each week—it might, for example, have been 'half a crown' (ie two shillings and six pence, equivalent to 12½p)—so that a nice

WHATEVER THE WEATHER . . .

The early months of 1947 have passed into UK weather folklore because of one of the harshest winters on record. Snow fell, and with sub-zero temperatures holding, the country came near to a total shut-down for some 2-3 months. Ledbury was snowed in and Little Marcle Road was impassable. After the initial snowfall, the lorry drivers had to dig the road clear so that business could carry on — not as usual, but at least after a fashion.

Flooding of the River Leadon was another potential problem, both in the 1940s and later in the 1950s and 60s — this was in the days before the by-pass was built with a consequent easing of the flood problem. Cut off from the rest of the town, one member of staff recalls risking it by driving her car along the crown of the road, and so getting into the factory to the amazement of all concerned. Staff who walked to work had bigger problems, and on at least one occasion, the factory's flat-back lorries were used to ferry people through the flood waters.

This was in an era though, when staff were simply expected to get to work with few excuses seen as acceptable. One employee remembers setting out for work, finding the road flooded and going back home to put on wellington boots — only to be told off when eventually reaching the factory for arriving late!

In the days before having your own car was the norm, there were a variety of ways of getting to work. Many staff lived in the town and so could — weather permitting — walk to the factory. Those from the surrounding towns and villages used other means: cycling was not unusual, with some quite long distances (from Colwall, Dymock or Much Marcle) being accepted as the price to pay for a good job at a good factory. At least one person travelled by train from Hereford, paying over one shilling in fares each day out of her £3-a-week wages, but hoping to be met at Ledbury station by someone with a car — or failing that a works lorry!

little pot of money was ready when the festive season arrived. However, the company's generosity was somewhat limited; they merely looked after this money and did not add any bonus or interest to it!

A longer-term staff benefit was to be the introduction of a pension scheme. Again, while the exact details of the Ledbury scheme are not known, it is likely that it followed that of D Jones Dickinson where 'a long discussion took place in regard to the installation of a pension scheme for all employees. After discussion, it was decided in the first place to consider a scheme not including any of the women'. Given the staff profile of Ledbury Preserves, this would probably have excluded most of the staff!

Occasional dinners open to all staff were also held, although mathematics does not seem to have been a strong suit: the 'Twenty-first Anniversary Dinner' was held in February 1950, while the Silver Anniversary meal was in 1953. Undeniably, these were worthy landmarks for Ledbury Preserves (1928) Ltd. They had survived the original bankruptcy and near closure, the economic depression of the 1930s, a world war and the death of two key members of staff in the 1940s. To celebrate these landmark achievements, celebratory dinners were held at a Gloucester hotel, and the future toasted. However, under the surface all was not well and the company was later to be described as being 'in a perilous condition'. It was a time of huge nationwide social and economic change and Ledbury Preserves would not be immune.

Carnival

With the end of the war, Ledbury once again had a summer carnival, and an entry from Ledbury Preserves was to become a regular feature.

An entry around 1946 or 1947 featured a tribute to the Land Army Girls (see facing page) who had kept the agricultural scene—and hence the jam factory—going through those difficult times. Other floats featured a 'welcome home' to the men from the services, or more frivolous subjects such as gollies (see above).

Office Life in the Forties

Violet Mowberry worked at the factory as a switchboard operator from 1945. The switchboard was of the old fashioned wooden box style, with wires that had to be plugged into sockets to make a connection. She had to be polite when answering an incoming call, and staff making an outgoing call would contact her and ask for a line. While the post was delivered to the factory, it was not collected, and she (or one of the other members of staff) would have to take the outgoing mail to the Post Office in the town—then on the corner of Bank Crescent—on their way home; a task that was not always easy when you had come to work on your bike.

The office itself was, as now, at the front of the factory, adjoining the Little Marcle Road, but was little more than a lean-to, with no external entry door of its own. Ruth Edwards (who joined in 1954) recalls that firstly you had to go through a 'step over' door into the lorry loading bay, and then

The original office building

along a concrete corridor open to the factory on your left, and with a wooden partition on your right; at the far end, there was a door from the factory into the sanctuary of the office. However, the partition wall was thin, and so the office could be quite a noisy place as the sounds of the factory came through. In this partition between factory and office was a glass panel and a hatch; visitors or factory staff needing the office would knock on this, and the office staff would slide the hatch to one side to speak to whoever was there and—if appropriate—then open the door for them.

Beryl Davenport first joined the company in 1947, doing almost anything that needed doing, whether this was typing or checking in the supplies being delivered. She reported to Miss Davis, a very prim and proper lady who looked after the girls—around eight of them—in the main office. Both she and Monica Jones (who joined in 1946) recall the rigmarole if you needed to spend a penny. The only toilet was an outside one, and you first had to ask for the key, before again going out of the office, along the concrete corridor, through the loading bay and back out using the 'step over' door, running

The new office block circa 1960. People in the picture include Ricky Southern (back left) with Walter Hodges next to him.

the gauntlet as you did so of rude comments from the factory girls who had gone outside for a cigarette!

The etiquette of the 1940s and 50s was very different to current trends. First names would never be used and apart from your own close friends, you always addressed people as Mr or Mrs So-and-so.

The office itself had its problems. For a start, it was on a slant and the floor sloped. If even chairs could end up where they hadn't been placed, then anything lighter that was accidentally dropped on the floor would roll away and start a grand game of chase the pencil. It was not until much later, after Avana had acquired control, that a new office block was built.

The factory seems to have had a canteen from the outset. The 1923 auction papers mentioned in Chapter 1 refer to a 'meal room', and since the Callan's wedding reception was held there in 1931, there must have been some form of catering facility at that time. In the post-war years, it is the menu of mince and veg followed by some form of milk pudding that still sticks in people's minds! It was also used as a place to serve tea to visiting tour parties. It was still there to the end of the factory's jam making life and provided a place for all staff from all levels to meet together and socialise, as well as eat.

Naming the Product

This 1969 advert designed for the export market shows jams and preserves marketed simply as 'Ledbury'. While many products were specifically made as own label brands, there were several other in-house marketing names over the years.

The 1944 D Jones Dickinson AGM refers to 'the well known Malvern Hills brand of jams'.

At that time, there was also a brand called Wyevern and in the late 1960s, there was a 'Belle Orchard' label, named after a street in Ledbury—this was aimed at the cheaper end of the market.

4 ❦ The Avana Era

Under New Management

It was the period under the ownership of Avana which brought Ledbury Preserves from being a small local company into the modern era as part of a major food manufacturing group. Avana's heart was in its bakery operations, initially in Cardiff and subsequently expanding to include a large modern site on the outskirts of Newport. The Welsh financier, Julian Hodge, became a member of the board in the early 1950s and he and his associates acquired a significant shareholding. The business was close to collapse and he employed astute financial management to get the company back on its feet. He also sought to address the poor business situation by advocating a programme of rationalisation and expansion. This led, in 1956, to the acquisition of its rival, D Jones Dickinson Ltd, which, as we have seen, owned and also purchased bakery jams from Ledbury Preserves.

The profitable years that Ledbury Preserves had enjoyed in the thirties and forties were now history and the silver anniversary celebrations of 1953 could not mask the fact that the business was in difficulties. Ownership of Ledbury Preserves was not something that Avana had, as such, sought; it was simply an unavoidable implication of its strategically logical decision to rationalise cake supply into Marks & Spencer and the South Wales valleys. Hence, ownership of Ledbury Preserves represented a real and pressing problem for Avana. In an effort to resolve this, Hodge approached his established cake customer, Marks & Spencer, for an order. Ledbury Preserves had supplied jams in both 1lb and 2lb jars to M&S in the 1930s but possibly this arrangement had lapsed in the face of the restrictions and other disruptions of World War II. Whatever had happened in the intervening period, Hodge was now told that provided the jam was made from fresh fruit, they would be prepared to give it a trial run. For this, he needed £75,000 immediately to buy fruit, a sum which was beyond the then independent lending authority of any of his banking connections in Cardiff. In desperation, he telephoned the head office of Lloyds Bank in London and asked to speak to the chief general manager, whoever that might be. The man in question, E J Hill, duly came on the line and listened quietly to an exposition of the problem. At length, he asked what sort of fruit the £75,000

Initially Ledbury was the only non-cake business within Avana. We didn't really want it because it was such a seasonal business. In the summer there were dozens of women plugging strawberries. The place was like a brewery, with barrels everywhere and their own coopers.

While initially we wanted to dispose of Ledbury Preserves, the business, during part of the 1960s, became highly profitable, more profitable than the bakeries and consideration was given to the idea of floating it on the London Stock Exchange as a separate company. As an alternative, we also considered growth through acquisitions and discussions were held with the owners of T W Beach, Samuel Moore's of Devizes, Duerrs and Nelsons of Aintree. Ledbury Preserves didn't supply jam to Avana Bakeries before we acquired it but it did supply hundreds of tonnes each year in the sixties and early seventies when the Rogerstone bakery was heavily involved in the manufacture of both full size and mini swiss rolls because one kilo of jam was required for 130 swiss rolls!

Because Avana's first interest was the bakery, the jam business was largely managed from Ledbury itself and Avana personnel were only involved in certain negotiations with Marks & Spencer and in major purchases, both capital and revenue. The Ledbury Management indulged in lots of 'hero budgeting' and piecemeal capital expenditure. They had to come to us at Avana Group for capital. Imric Jagan was the main driver—a good technical man but sharp. A typical example concerns the replacement of the boilers which was presented to us as a 'must have' since the business possessed inadequate steam capacity to cope with growing demand for its products. Once this was accepted and we had approved the expenditure, the Ledbury management came back to us and said 'we now need more money because we've got nowhere to put the increased production'.

was required to buy. 'Raspberries sir? That's an awful lot of raspberries, Mr Hodge'. The money was to hand within twenty-four hours and so Ledbury Preserves survived to fight another day.

However, Avana's real interest lay in the Dowlais bakery. Avana's bakery made large cakes for distribution through its van sales operation and to Marks & Spencer while D Jones Dickinson supplied a largely identical customer base with small cakes. So the two businesses were complementary and were the major focus of attention for the directors of Avana. Therefore, they sold D Jones Dickinson's wholesaling operations in Cardiff and Llanelli and would almost certainly have sold Ledbury Preserves if a suitable buyer could have been identified because they found, in particular, that its seasonal demands for fruit sourcing and financing did not sit comfortably with the immediacy of the cake business.

Until the late 1970s, the Avana Group effectively had three divisions:
• The South Wales bakery operation producing private label cakes for major retailers, most notably Marks & Spencer.
• Ledbury Preserves, manufacturing bakery and retail jams.
• A Midlands-based savoury business purchased in 1964 which manufactured meat pies and pasties and would, in the 1980s, be the creator of the then revolutionary concept of chilled recipe dishes. This traded as two separate companies, R F Brookes and Avana Meat Products.

The link with Avana's bakeries was the one that was significant for Ledbury Preserves because it provided an outlet for its bakery jams. This was particularly important at a time when many independent bakers were being bought up by two major groups, Associated British Foods and, ironically, Ranks Hovis

McDougall. This 'hoovering up' of medium sized bakeries into groups which owned their own jam manufacturing operations progressively restricted the market available for Ledbury's bakery jams which had been the mainstay of the business twenty years earlier.

Swinging into the Sixties

Business with Avana Bakeries was, however, not large enough to sustain Ledbury Preserves and so as the fifties drew to an end, Avana extended Ledbury's functional skills by bringing in a specialist technical director, Imric Jagan, who was a Hungarian and a food scientist and F H (Ricky) Southern, a professional salesman with a Lever Brothers background. Between them, they drove two crucial strands of development:

Ricky Southern expanded the customer base within the arena of retail jams. While the business with M&S was retained, it was always handled by the managing director. Ricky's task was to seek out new opportunities within the then dominant voluntary groups and the small, but growing, multiples.

Imric Jagan was something of an innovator and was responsible for the introduction of vacuum boiling and the installation in the mid sixties of the APV plant, a continuous evaporation process which was perfect for long runs of smooth jams and fillings and which continued in use until 2008. Hence, it was ideally suited for another of his developments—the introduction of fifteen hundredweight stainless steel tanks as a method of supplying bakeries with high volume jams. Until this introduction, bakery jams had traditionally been supplied in 28lb tins with slip-on lids

FROM THE FIFTIES TO THE 21ST CENTURY: Ian Wheeler's Story

Ian started work at Ledbury Preserves in 1956, shortly after his fifteenth birthday, and spent all his working life there. He joined as office boy on £2.48 for a thirty-seven-and-a-half-hour week but to supplement this, he worked for many years on an evening shift in the factory from 6pm to 10pm, working on a capping machine at the time that the new 'rolltop' cans were introduced. Later he moved to the order desk.

Everything was filled into tins of various sizes. The main Marks & Spencer lines at the time were packed in 24 ounce tins with a wrap round label and these were the only jams with a significantly different specification, because of the M&S insistence on quality. There was an active relationship with D Jones Dickinson through supplying bakery jams to their Dowlais plant. There was, however, no cooling machinery. Typically, 1,500 tins were left to cool on the floor overnight and the first job in the morning was to clear and seal the tins from the previous day. Mincemeat was put down in barrels and decanted into tins when orders came in.

Woolworths was a big customer in the 1960s. Orders would come in from up to 300 stores and Ian would have to type up each order individually. The deliveries were sent by train from Ledbury to a central depot, including jam for Woolworths in Ledbury. Other customers—and there were many of them because the company was prepared to label up so-called 'bright' stock with low minimum orders—were supplied via a fleet of twenty-four lorries.

When Ian started work, the factory was driven on coal-fired boilers with coal initially coming from the Forest of Dean and then when the mines there closed, from Cannock. Every so often, the youngest or smallest boy—and Ian filled both criteria—would be required to work on a Saturday morning to clean the flues.

Sugar was delivered in bags and was set hard, often needing a sledgehammer to break it up! At harvest time, 1,000 tonnes or more of plums and apples would arrive and be processed and treated with sulphur dioxide, stored in barrels at the top of the yard and used as required. There were three types of plum which needed separating, yellow, red and the local Blaisdons which were considered to be the best. To service the barrels, three coopers were employed on site, working at the back of the boilers: Harry Hodges, Harry Carpenter and Teddy Smith.

which were a nightmare to stack and must have presented huge problems of disposal. A medium sized bakery, using around 250 tonnes of jam in a year, would have no less than 400 tins to trash every week! Management of waste was, in fact, becoming increasingly important both to customers and to Ledbury Preserves itself. Originally, the jam factory simply dumped its effluent in the River Leadon but it is suggested that, after this practice resulted in the death of 'a couple of cows', something more had to be done. This explains why the Ledbury Preserves site of twenty-seven acres was so much more extensive than the factory's needs would appear to dictate because fields were bought so that effluent could be sprayed over them! Eventually a deal was done with the local council for the company to contribute substantially to the building of a new treatment plant which would serve both the town and the jam factory.

On the customer front, the trading philosophy from the mid-fifties onwards was to win private label sales which Ricky Southern always described as 'the cream of the business'. The company did, in fact, run three brands but they were largely default options for customers too small to warrant a private label of their own—and they had to be very small to fall into this category! Of these three brands, the one which genuinely had a unique position was the 'Ledbury' range of conserves and good quality marmalades in 'rolltop' cans. This very attractive, unusual and table-ready packaging featured a pale blue Wedgwood design and probably, if it had been marketed consistently, could have come to rival Tiptree at the luxury end of the preserves market. However, problems in generating sufficient volume to print the large quantities of cans that their manufacturer required meant that the range was discontinued by the late seventies.

Another feature of the customer end of the business that would now seem very unusual was that the selling throughout the sixties was largely undertaken either by Ricky Southern himself or by sales agents, of whom there were at one time thirty-two. They were allocated a geographical area of the country and were responsible for all business therein, whether to bakeries, wholesalers or retailers. These men—and they always were men, normally 'of a certain age'—were paid typically a percentage of the invoice value of whatever they sold. Thus, it was argued that, if they failed to do very much effective work, at least they did not cost the company very much. The downside, of course, was that if they did not secure available business, it went to a competitor. Hence, Ledbury Preserves' sales across the country were very patchy. Anything north of the Wash and east of the Pennines was virtually unknown territory and Ricky Southern was particularly ambivalent about attempting to do business in Scotland. Just getting there by car must have been an extraordinarily convoluted journey in pre-motorway days and so it was his opinion that everything north of Hadrian's Wall would be better towed out into the North Sea and sunk!

The recruitment in 1962 of Roy Poole, subsequently the company's personnel manager, as an 'Executive' is also illustrative of how matters were handled at that time. He had previously worked for a rival company, Ticklers, as a jam salesman but saw takeovers coming and so placed his details with an agency which arranged an interview for him with Avana in Cardiff. No one from Ledbury was involved in either the interview or the appointment process! Following his somewhat ambiguous appointment, he underwent a two week induction at Avana Bakeries and was then taken to Ledbury Preserves where he met Walter Hodges for the first time. He was, however, clearly destined for great things as he was one of the few people to be bought a new desk! This was placed in a corner of Hodges' office. Within a short time, Poole concluded that the company was 'totally disorganised' with no proper reporting structure; it seemed that everyone reported to Hodges on just about every issue.

As an extreme example of this, Jack was the maintenance fitter who looked after the company's lorries. He wore a blue boiler suit but his face and hands were always covered in black oil and grease. Since all decisions were taken by Hodges, Jack would come into the office and say 'the halfshaft of the Pegler's broke'. Hodges would ask how much a new one would cost, say it was too much and they ended up cannibalising some other lorry! When Jack was ill and had to take several months off work, a stand-in was recruited. Towards the end of his illness, Jack looked in at the factory and immediately pointed out that the stand-in

MODERNISING THE FACTORY: A View from Mike McQuaid who joined in 1964 and stayed until his retirement in 2005

I came from a heavy engineering business in Hereford. By comparison with what I had been used to, Ledbury Preserves was very friendly. Once you were accepted, which took about twelve months, it was like a family. Everyone accepted everyone else and everyone knew everyone else's business. It was just a very friendly place. I joined as assistant plant engineer, intending to spend about two years there but I was so impressed, I decided to stay.

When I joined, there were open pans all the way across the building, separated into what were called A, B and C Sections. The A Section Vacuum Pans replaced the old Open Pans. B Section was where E Section was subsequently sited. Mincemeat was produced on the mezzanine floor.

The sixties were a terrific time to work at the company. The APV, A Section and High Level Boiling vessels were installed in quick succession, making Ledbury Preserves, at that time, the most modern jam factory in Europe.

WHO SAID ROLL OUT THE BARREL ?

Barrels, barrels, everywhere -and not a drop of beer—or der! The barrels shown in ur photograph are at Ledbury reserves (1928) Ltd, and were ied in their day to transport esh fruit to the factory. But once again the old has make way for the new, and

the sight of barrels is becoming even more scarce. In the background of our photograph can be seen the circular ends of huge new storage tanks where up to 100 tons of fruit pulp per tank can be stored. But modern mechanisation

has not taken over fruit trans- portation completely, and some of the old barrels are still used on occasion. Our photograph shows maintenance man Mr Gerald Hanford inspecting the wooden veterans — just in case they are called for.

was actually repairing people's cars in the yard in company time!

If stories such as these prompt questions as to how the company could have none-theless survived and grown, it is worth reflecting on the fact that its disciplines were probably no worse than those of many other contemporary medium sized food businesses. In fact, almost twenty years later, the family that owned Robertson's, the largest preserves manufacturer in the UK, was to demonstrate a different sort of disorganisation in that it possessed scant knowledge of the Avana Group despite the fact that it owned a competing preserves business.

Hence, Ledbury Preserves continued to develop its operations and by the early 1970s the layout of the jam factory that will be familiar to those who worked in Ledbury in later years was established. An extensive 'farm' of 100 tonne holding tanks had largely replaced the barrels and their coopers. The Fruit Processing Department handled all raw and frozen fruit and ran two vacuum boiling pans which were used for making concentrates and some industrial products. The fresh citrus plant did not yet exist and the tank farm at the rear of the site was very extensive as virtually all jams, other than those made either directly or indirectly for Marks & Spencer, were produced from fruit preserved in evil-smelling sulphur dioxide. Within the main jam factory, products could be processed under vacuum on 'A Section'; in an enclosed high temperature boiling process at 'High Level'; via the APV continuous evaporation plant or on 'B Section' which was the least sophisticated of the processes. B Section consisted of six open copper pans, essentially large saucepans, from which products were decanted once fully boiled by tilting into open troughs before being pumped away for filling. There were two lines for filling glass jars while industrial preserves could be packed into 12½ kilo buckets, cartons or pails, 25 kilo pails or moveable tanks. There were also facilities for can-ning in small 'iron ration' packs for sale under contract to the War Office and in a tin called an A10 which was used for the late 1960s and early 1970s'

expansion into 'yogfruit' for yoghurt manufacture. The latter line of business had faded away by the late 1970s because dairy technology had moved forward and required aseptic packing of 25 kilo units, something that was beyond Ledbury Preserves' capability.

Rubber-lined 100-tonne-capacity fruit storage tanks

Diversification

This era also saw another development which was to be hugely important for Ledbury Preserves. Driven by Imric Jagan, the company began experimenting with the manufacture of fruit juice. The sixties must have seen the development of technology in locations such as Florida, Mexico and Brazil which permitted freshly squeezed orange juice to be concentrated, pasteurised and packed into steel drums. This material, around six times the strength of normal orange juice, could then be frozen and shipped to other parts of the world much more cheaply than ready to drink juice because of the massive reduction of its volume.

Jagan was a great traveller and visited many countries to source fruits for jam. Probably in the course of this work, he came across some of the earliest juice concentrate offerings and had samples brought back to Ledbury. There, they were simply reconstituted by the addition of water, pasteurised by being boiled on 'B Section' as if they were jams and then hot filled into

Vacuum boiling:
15 cwt batches produced
under vacuum to retain
natural fruit flavours

tall jars. By 1973, Avana had invested to update and expand this Heath-Robinson process and had created a bespoke fruit juice processing plant using a heat exchanger similar to that which sat at the heart of the continuous evaporation jam plant and an effective, but slow, bottling line located in the area where, more recently, mobile tanks were filled. This was followed by the introduction of long-life, aseptic cartoning using the now common 'Tetrapak' technology. At that time, however, it was very new and Ledbury's Tetrapak plant was only the third in the UK. This was very different and unfamiliar technology which used a different heating principle (induction heating) and computer controls. Mike McQuaid recalls going to visit the supplier in Sweden in 1971 and said he'd never been so cold in his life!

The fruit juice operation was to grow and grow until, by the end of the decade, it had become not only the dominant business within Ledbury Preserves but also the most visible part of Avana Group's operations. This story deserves a chapter of its own and so Chapter 7 will develop a

picture of the growth, flowering and sad decline of fruit juice production in Ledbury.

In the meantime, however, such extensions to both plant and product ranges gradually dictated the need for better disciplines in the workplace. In the mid-sixties, the company's only nod in the direction of security was the employment of a night-watchman; the police used to regularly look in on him as he was always ready with a cup of tea for them. This arrangement was ultimately expanded into a team of four security men, two for the day shift and two for nights. The day shift

In the sixties fork-lift trucks reduced manual handling—here Brian Wall shows off his truck and his chest

consisted of ex-policemen (former tea-drinkers?) who also logged all vehicle movements and manned the phones before the receptionist arrived and after she left. When staff lockers were introduced in the early seventies, the security staff held duplicate keys since employees would often lose their key or forget to bring it with them. Another consequence of the introduction of lockers was the end of 'the three minute trot'. The arrangement had been that staff had three minutes from clock-on time to change into work clothes and get into the factory. However, the clocks were in the factory, and so staff used to go into the factory as they arrived, then come out and use the allotted three minutes to change and get back in again! Thus, for example, if they clocked on at 8.30 am, they had to be on the production line by 8.33 am. This cumbersome procedure was repeated at lunch time and when clocking off, so twelve minutes were lost to production every day. Negotiations took place which resulted in an agreement that staff had to be on the job by their start time but to compensate, the factory stopped at 4 pm rather than 5 pm on Fridays. It also meant that staff were not allowed into the factory unless properly dressed in protective clothing.

In the mid-seventies, a series of management changes took place which were to prove highly significant for both Ledbury Preserves and Avana. The company had been run since the time of World War II by Walter Hodges, who lived next door to the factory, in a number of wide-ranging senior roles and finally as managing director.

He retired in 1974 and the occasion was marked with a grand party at the Feathers Hotel (see above) but his immediate replacement did not stay the course.

Although Hodges returned to do a holding job for six months, Avana had appointed Dr John Randall, previously production director of Nestlé UK, as a consultant. Both Avana and Ledbury Preserves were, at this time, struggling financially. Jam profitability had been low since the late sixties and although fruit juice sales were taking off, a combination of inadequate pricing and high production costs associated with shift working to meet booming demand, meant that the company was hardly breaking even. Randall's job, initially within Ledbury and subsequently within Avana, was to challenge existing practices and bring the businesses back into profitability.

Randall became Ledbury's managing director in 1976 and managing director of Avana Group two years later. He was far from content with what he found and ran the businesses in a very distinctive style. It was often said that his office was his Mercedes and he would turn up at factories, without prior warning, at completely unexpected times, maybe at weekends or at 5.30 in the evening when most people had gone home. He thus saw what was really happening and who was really doing the work, rather than accepting at face value, an image carefully nurtured by the management of the businesses. There was therefore a flurry of management changes, with John Mitchell, who had been company secretary at Avana Bakeries, becoming the bakery's managing director and Andrew Bonnett, a young accountant who had held a similar role at Ledbury, becoming initially its general manager and subsequently in 1981, its managing director. John Randall had little time for the trappings of big companies so company directors were few in number, no PR or advertising agencies were used and while there was a major focus on innovation, this was done using internal resources—and these included Mrs Randall's kitchen—rather than outside consultancies. At the same time, he recognised the needs of the factory personnel and so undertook a major investment to provide modern canteen, locker-room and changing facilities.

Thus, both the Avana Group and Ledbury Preserves acquired a new vigour and an enthusiasm for the rapid introduction of profitable new products. For Ledbury, the relationship with Marks & Spencer and the fruit juice business fitted this profile but it proved much harder to innovate in the much more traditional bakery and private label jam businesses. Innovation in these two areas was also hampered by the fact that, apart from Marks & Spencer, most customers were very definitely second or third division operators. Retail jam provides the best example of this, where the biggest customer from the late 1960s to the mid-1970s was the Spar-Vivo Voluntary Group. Today, Spar is a very small player in the UK grocery market but at that

AVANA AND LEDBURY PRESERVES: The initial perception of Dr John Randall

Dr John Randall was initially approached by Sir Julian Hodge but he came first on a consultancy basis because he had doubts about the business. Moving to Ledbury Preserves from a large multinational business, where he had 10,700 people working directly or indirectly for him, entailed entering a completely different world! Dr Randall specifically came to work at Ledbury Preserves, initially in 1974. He was then later asked to become a director when the then managing director was moved out suddenly, and he became managing director the following year. Two years later he was appointed managing director of the Avana Group. When he joined Avana it was in trouble, with a market capitalisation of only £902,000. Tom Barrett would arrange to present the accounts to shareholders on a Christmas Eve to minimise the risk of angry confrontations.

Also, there were various dubious practices taking place at Ledbury. Shortly after Randall joined, there was a poor local plum harvest and he had to contend with rowdy local farmers who, for the first time, found their fruit rejected on quality grounds. Previously, this fruit would have been accepted, probably with some 'incentives' being paid. As a result of this new and decisive stance, product quality improved.

time, it was bigger than Tesco and the weekly preserves manufacturing programme was never produced until the Spar order had arrived in Ledbury, such was its importance. Its buying director was a figure so fear-inspiring that Ricky Southern would cross himself before taking a phone call from him!

5 ◁ 'Start Right Away If You Want'—!

The years from 1962 onward in Britain are usually characterised as the 'swinging sixties', an era of great social change and technological advance. Harold Wilson's Labour government granted MBEs to The Beatles and established a Ministry of Technology under Tony Benn to exploit the 'white heat' of scientific and industrial advances.

However, it took some time for that 'white heat' to percolate across the Cotswolds, along the A417 and into Little Marcle Road. One reason may have been that few of the supervisors and management had any experience outside the preserves industry and many had only ever worked at Ledbury Preserves. Annie Roberts, who started her long career at Ledbury as the sixties ended, noted that 'When I started, there were no computers and I don't think there was any manager who hadn't worked his way up from the bottom. Then David Smith and Andrew Bonnett were recruited and they did great things to modernise and push the business forward'.

Nonetheless, Ledbury Preserves seems always to have had a 'good feel' to it, with good working relationships between staff and management. It has often been said that it was like 'a large family.' This meant that staff problems were generally few and far between. For example, in the sixties, PA Management Consultants were asked to look at the way the company was run and one issue they identified was the need for 'work study', also known as 'time and motion study' and a much-used management buzzword at that time. The introduction of 'the man with the clipboard' had been a stumbling block in many other companies but because it was linked to a bonus system, it did not create problems in Ledbury. The union representative, John George, was well respected by the workforce; he was brought on side first and made part of the initial work study team. When he appeared with the inevitable clipboard, it was accepted by the workforce and so 'standard times' needed to produce goods could be worked out. If a production line exceeded this '100 per cent level' they got a bonus; for example, if they produced ten per cent more jam than standard, then they got a bonus of ten per cent in their wages. The work study team was to expand, eventually having seven people on this and work flow studies.

Strikes were virtually unknown although Polly Sturge, who first joined the company in 1959, recalls that a brief downing of tools took place in May 1960. The occasion was the marriage of Princess Margaret. A television set had been made available so that the office staff could view the nuptials, which went down badly with the rest of the workforce and provoked a brief stoppage. Gerald Hanford recalls that he was working inside a tank and when he emerged, none of his colleagues was anywhere to be seen. He eventually found them on strike in the canteen. Apparently, the dispute was resolved when the television in the office was removed, although by then, the royal knot had presumably been tied. There was another short spell of industrial action in the late sixties or early seventies, when there was a dispute over wages. There were pickets outside the factory and all vehicles entering or leaving were stopped. However, this did not have the wholehearted support of the workforce and it fizzled out after a couple of days, with no marked effect on factory operations, although a management attempt to stop overtime as a punitive measure proved counterproductive and had to be withdrawn when they ended up with fresh strawberries rotting in the yard.

So in many ways, Ledbury Preserves was a different place in which to work—friendly, family-oriented and changing only gradually. Clearly, as the climate for food manufacturing became more competitive and the regulatory demands greater, things would have to change for the business to survive. But before we move on to the era of rapid change, it is worth looking at the recollections of two men who provided the characteristic diligent and loyal work that sustained the business for so long. Both Gerald Hanford and David Sturge spent over forty years working at The Pozzy.

Gerald Hanford:

'After I left school, I worked on farms for three years. I first went to the jam factory when I was nineteen. When I asked about a job I was asked 'When do you want to start? You can start right away if you want.' I still had my regular clothes on but I started then and there on the spot and I stayed for over forty years! I used to work in a gang unloading lorries by hand. The sugar was supplied in bags in those days; the brown sugar, especially, was as hard as concrete. That is one example of how much of our work then was physically very hard. Another example is that for a while, I was the relief stoker, shovelling coal into the boilers. The whole yard used to be covered with ashes from the boilers, with the exception of a small concreted area where glass was unloaded.

Handling fruit also demanded long hours of unrelenting and difficult work. In the fruit season, we would receive hundreds of boxes of plums, apples and strawberries in particular. We never used to wash the fruit; it was just sieved. Fruit which was not made into jam immediately was filled into barrels with sulphur dioxide. Although it was hazardous and smelt terrible, we didn't take precautions such as wearing masks; we just tried to stay upwind. Once we had done our work, the team of three coopers would come after us sealing

Gerald Hanford with his tractor

the barrels. The following day we would stack the barrels; that was a very tough job and by the time we had finished, our backs were aching. Strawberries used to come from Wisbech, arriving at 6.00 am and a team of women would sort them for processing; anything left unsorted at 4.00 pm would be put into barrels with sulphur dioxide.

It was not considered necessary for those of us who worked outside to wear protective clothing; in fact we would work outside in the summer without shirts on, with wasps all around, but I was only ever stung once! On the other hand, there were some very cold winters and then we would burn old barrels to keep the frost off and thaw the pipes!

I was responsible for the meadow where the barrels were stored; I was the last of the yard men but they still used to call me 'the boy.' There had been fifteen of us when I started, plus more casual employees in the season. At the beginning, I had an old 1949 Bedford lorry with a tail lift. Later I had two tractors, and then fork lift trucks took over. Although the work was hard, I was happy. We were a lot happier then because when it gets mechanical, it gets boring. There were no rules so we used to get up to all sorts of mischief. There were also lots of romances; I met my wife at the factory.'

David Sturge:

'When I had my job interview, it was with the then managing director, Walter Hodges. There were no CVs back then; in those days word of mouth was good enough to secure employment. I was taken on as a yard hand. This job included a variety of duties, one of which was the unloading of bags of dry sugar via a conveyer belt into what later became known as the High-Level Boiling Room. In those days, there was no delivery of road-tanker syrup; we produced our own in the High-Level Boiling Area in two large

Gerald Hanford
and Brian Wall
in the early 1960s

vats and dropped it down into cloth filters in what was eventually known as the Colour Room.

During the apple and plum season it was a time of high activity; trucks, tractors and trailers would line up back on to the main road to unload their fruit, much of it packed in wooden trays or boxes. At these times of year, processing of fruits took place seven days per week. The work was done on a large wooden platform with boiling vats that were injected with steam. Fruit would be tipped into the boiling vat, water added and the mix brought to a boil. Then the steam would be shut off and the fruit, now known as pulp, would be put through a sieve to extract stones and pips before being stored in barrels just as Gerald Hanford has described.

It was not long before I transferred into the main factory. My first encounter was with Harry Hill who was the jam foreman. It was clear from the start, he was a significant figure and knew his job. I had to learn the mysteries of open pan boiling and how to operate filling machines. Harry had a few special boiling pans which he used for lemon and orange curds. Filling and sealing of jars was done by hand on a round rotary wooden table. On a Friday night after the week's work was done, Harry would give us a whistle. This was the signal to go to the cooper's shop to sample the home-made cider which we had produced from surplus apples during the previous mincemeat season!

Jams were made using traditional methods on open copper pans. The plant known as 'B Section' consisted of six pans each located on top of its own iron bowl, which provided the energy source: steam injection. The boiling pans sat on a framework axis which enabled the pan to be tipped forward by hand into a cooling tray, which in turn was connected to pipe work through which the product could be pumped to various filling lines.

The term 'handball' was often used at that time but it had nothing to do with football! Instead, it described the fact that almost everything was moved by hand. There was no pumping or metering of ingredients so the drums or barrels were 'handballed' across the yard by men hauling a small trolley. Each fruit ingredient was ladled from a barrel into a bowl and weighed and then manually lifted into the boiling pan. The other main ingredient, sugar-syrup, was semi-weighed and loaded by the boiler and then the small ingredients such as acids, citrate, colours and pectins were added. The loading of fruits into open boiling pans was not a pleasant job.

Fruits were preserved with sulphur dioxide and loading next to open pans of boiling jam was a tricky task. Burns from the hot jam were not unknown and, unsurprisingly, the regular footwear around the boiling area was clogs.

Each 'boil' had an output of about 150 lbs (68 kilos). Once all the ingredients were loaded, boiling commenced with steam turned on to each pan at five minute intervals in order to create a continuous boiling pattern. The jam boilers worked from master recipes and one of the main targets was total soluble solids (TSS). Each boiler had a temperature gauge and during boiling, would take a sample and test the TSS, continuing to do so until the target was reached while keeping a watchful eye on the temperature gauge. The master recipe was tiny compared with modern recipe files and not so complex and demanding. Technical knowledge has moved on over the years, particularly at bakeries, and as a result, achieving specified qualities in the final product is now much more critical.

The boiling section was versatile and could supply various filling lines, although not simultaneously. The major filling lines handled 28 lb cartons and tins and 7 lb tins. Once these containers were filled, they were trucked away and left to cool and set overnight. There was no automated cooling of products in those days. So the next day, all of the cooled and set jams had to be packed, stacked and the tins had to be lidded. Cartons were taped by hand and stacked. The quantity some days was in excess of a thousand units.'

Getting Staff

With around 200 people on the books, it could be difficult getting staff — not surprising when you think that this probably represented around ten per cent of Ledbury's adult population at the time! Obviously, people came in from surrounding villages such as Colwall, Dymock and Much Marcle and they travelled in a variety of ways: on foot, by car, bike, bus, train and scooter. In the sixties and seventies, dedicated bus services ran for a while. There were three routes: two were operated by minibuses and came from Much Marcle and from the Newtown crossroads, while the third, a larger vehicle, came from Bosbury via the Market House in Ledbury's Lower Road, picking up town staff as it came. Staff paid a small charge to use one of these routes but the service was subsidised to a considerable extent. If recruiting and keeping regular staff was difficult, finding seasonal staff was a nightmare.

In the fruit picking season, the need for staff exploded and in particular, bulk supplies of strawberries had to be hulled. Buses were laid on from wherever people could be found willing to do the work: Gloucester, Leominster or Hereford for example. These were often mums who would bring their children with them, children who should, in some cases, have been at school. Roy Poole, the company's personnel manager, recalls on one occasion that the head of a secondary school arrived at the factory in his car and marched purple-faced into the factory, disregarding the hygiene and protective clothing rules, to identify his missing pupils. One incentive tried for a year was to set up a crèche for the younger children; this was held at what was the St John Ambulance headquarters in the Southend (near to the Royal Oak public house). The coach would drop the children there, then bring mums on to the factory. In the evening, it would pick up the children first, then collect mums—but on one occasion, the evening coach was found to be one child short. Fortunately, he was still at St John's HQ, a person tidying up having found him! A major problem was that a meal had to be provided for the children and so the difficulties mounted. Overall, it was felt that the problems outweighed the benefits and the Ledbury Preserves crèche ran for just one year!

What It Was Like: An Overview and A Spot Of Socialising

In the course of researching this book, a considerable number of employees and ex-employees have been interviewed and very many of them have commented that Ledbury Preserves was a very friendly place to work—although some of them have also commented that it had to be friendly to retain staff because the wages were so poor! Mike McQuaid spoke for many when he described it as 'just a very friendly place'. As we saw above, Gerald Hanford recalled that as a young man, he found it a happy place to be and that he and his friends and colleagues used to get up to all sorts of mischief. Annie Roberts, who joined in 1970, was more direct: 'The pay was dreadful, they used to pay farm workers' wages. This led to a high staff turnover. Within eighteen months, I was the longest serving employee in the office. People could sometimes double their salary by moving to another employer. Belatedly, this was recognised and salaries did improve.'

Perhaps something of a compensation, especially in the sixties and for a few years subsequently, was that social activities had always had a place in Ledbury Preserves. From the charabanc outings of the 1930s, through Red Cross fund raising events of the 1940s, to the anniversary dinners of the 1950s, people enjoyed sharing each other's company. It was in the 1960s,

however, that these really took off. A social club was formed with a staff committee to carry ideas forward. These were wide-ranging and imaginative. There were Easter Bonnet parties and an annual dinner dance, carnival float entries and a fireworks party. The latter was held on the field behind the factory; a 'great big urn' was carried out, a light was somehow rigged up, and soup and sausages served. Anyone from the town could come and a small charge was made for admission. In later years, the idea was taken up by the Rotary Club and the Jam Factory Fireworks came to an end. There were also Christmas parties but one had to take care!! As autumn went, the juice from the crushed apples was saved to form the basis of a punch for the Christmas celebrations. However, people tended to add alcohol at random to this, and the concoction was potentially lethal! Jan Pearce, who worked at the factory for most of the 1960s, remembers being warned 'don't drink anything if it's not poured from a bottle'. In the seventies and eighties, Annie Roberts became secretary of the social club and recalls organising many events, although eventually the enthusiasm waned. Games of football or rounders against other local companies such as Chapman's and Spicers were arranged, followed of course, by a trip to the pub!

Easter Bonnet Dance at the Feathers Hotel 1974

6 ⁓ Avana, RHM & the James Robertson Years

Avana: From Favourite to Fallen Star

In 1974, Avana had been not far short of a dead duck. Its sales had risen by twenty per cent over the financial year to reach £12.7 million but massive inflation, poor business processes and the three day week were taking their toll; after tax and dividends had been paid, retained profits stood at only £32,000! All of Avana's three business streams were languishing and its shares, which were quoted on the London Stock Exchange, were trading at just £0.04. By 1980, that nadir had become a distant memory and Avana had become the darling of the Food sector. But darlings have to deliver and keep on delivering so John Randall started to look for appropriate bolt-on acquisitions. In that year, Nestlé put its Keiller marmalade operation up for sale and Randall and David Smith flew to Scotland to check it out. Randall did not proceed with this purchase and Keiller was sold to the delightfully named Okhai Group and, years later, was acquired as a brand by RHM. On the flight back, both men were studying brokers' circulars about publicly quoted food companies and Randall noted that Smith was particularly interested in a circular regarding the Robertson's Food Group.

Robertson's owned the ubiquitous jam brand, Golden Shred (Slogan: 'The world's most famous marmalade'), Viota cake mixes, a private label cereal manufacturing business, dried fruit merchanting, a Bristol-based wine kit manufacturer, vegetable canneries in France and a small chain of health food stores! They also owned the iconic Golly, the world's longest running consumer promotion and a corporate aeroplane which had the appropriate registration letters G-OLLY, piloted by Captain Andy Band. Both men realised that Robertson's was really trading on past glories and that greater efficiencies and drive could be brought into its operations. Randall therefore sought and won the backing of the Avana Board to mount an audacious take-over bid for a company twice Avana's size! Robertson's initially reacted with utter incredulity and publicly asked: 'Who are Avana?' However, they had done little to cultivate goodwill in the City, whereas brokers' visits had been a regular feature of life at Ledbury Preserves and other Avana companies for some time. The City was therefore willing to back Randall's vision and Avana succeeded in its bid and immediately trebled in size.

What should have been good news for Ledbury Preserves actually triggered a period of difficulty and uncertainty within its business. Almost simultaneously with the acquisition, the level of competitive activity in the fruit juice market had increased dramatically with the introduction of new and aggressive players within both the branded and private label sectors. Ledbury Preserves and the James Robertson operations in Droylsden were not integrated and so, while Ledbury was able to undertake work on the

Robertson's brand, there was no overall strategy to enable the two preserves businesses to access fully the benefits of a potentially stronger position in manufacturing, purchasing and selling. Management focus was therefore diluted and this became more pronounced as Avana made further acquisitions: a wafer-biscuit manufacturer, OP Chocolates, in South Wales and a bulk chocolate manufacturer, Lesme, based in Banbury. Avana also mounted an abortive takeover bid for Trebor Bassett which was subsequently swallowed up by Cadbury Schweppes. The failed bid did not help Avana's cause and its star began to wane. Investment was, entirely understandably, channelled to the most profitable and growing areas of Avana, notably private label cereal manufacturing and the burgeoning recipe dish and pizza business of R F Brookes. Hence, the only real benefit to Ledbury of the Robertson's acquisition was that it took on the packing of catering packs of preserves and the manufacture of a Robertson's sub-brand, Today's Recipe, which was designed to take advantage of a new opportunity created by the 1981 Jam Regulations to market in the UK for the first time, a range of low-sugar preserves. The downside was that capital for what had become once again a rather dull business was not forthcoming and so factory operations stagnated.

A New Name over the Door

Also stagnating was the Avana share price and Northern Foods, the majority shareholder with twenty per cent, became impatient and sold its share to RHM which used it as a platform in 1987 to mount a bid. The contested takeover process was quite dramatic for people at Ledbury. Avana fought this bid strongly and Ledbury Preserves' employees were encouraged to use car stickers with the message 'Don't let the millers grind you down'. The local MP was lobbied, mass meetings were held in the canteen and David

Smith, with Mike McQuaid one of the two Ledbury-based directors, went on local radio to explain why ownership by RHM would prove a disaster. He therefore found it rather difficult some weeks later, when the RHM bid proved successful, and he had to walk the RHM chairman round a quiet factory one Saturday morning!

The change of ownership inevitably had both positive and negative aspects. One of the latter, and something that was felt acutely by all employees, was the loss of the Avana share-ownership scheme. The Avana Group had already pushed employer pension contributions up to the limit of what was allowed by the Inland Revenue but one of Randall's favourite achievements, albeit the brainchild of finance director, Tom Barrett, was the Avana Group's profit-sharing scheme. This was an allocated rather than contributory scheme, applicable to every employee who had been with the company for over three years. It was highly valued by personnel at Ledbury Preserves, many of whom had decades of service behind them. Randall had explained to them that it was his desire that this scheme would deliver to them their most valuable asset apart from their house (assuming the latter was owned). It worked like this:

• Shares were purchased in the marketplace and allocated on the basis of a 'points' system in which length of service and salary featured.

• The annual value of shares allocated and initially held by trustees on behalf of the individuals ranged between £50 and £300 so that there was a fair degree of equity with both long-serving directors and recently arrived shop-floor workers seeing a valuable share allocation in their names.

• Ownership eventually transferred from the trustees to the individual employee after seven years.

While the loss of this scheme was keenly felt, there were upsides. The publicity surrounding the

HOW AVANA FELL TO RHM: some Avana Group insights from Tom Barrett

When Sir Julian Hodge and his associates left Avana, John Randall had hoped to buy twenty per cent shareholding which later became the platform for the RHM bid. However, the deterioration in their relationship precluded this and so this major shareholding was sold to Northern Foods.

John Randall and Chris, later Lord Haskins, then the chairman of Northern Foods, took seats on each other's boards but the relationship between the two companies which often squared up as competitors was never an easy one.

As Avana found it increasingly hard to maintain its previously hectic profit growth, Randall generated a plan for a new manufacturing facility, Dragon Parc, which was scuppered when Avana fell to RHM. If successful, the plan would have seen this huge site near to Merthyr converted into two highly efficient plants: one for cakes, one for savouries. The existing cake bakeries and Brookes/Avana Meat Products plants would have been folded into it and their existing sites sold. A two to three year payback was projected.

QUANTOCK:
An overview from Mike McQuaid

Quantock had three strands of business:

- Fresh Fruit Marmalade: we didn't need to use their kit but adapted our own.
- Jaffa: safe manufacture of Jaffa demands a continuous evaporation plant and three of these machines had been produced for the UK. Imric Jagan worked closely with APV on the first one to be built but the first actually to be installed was the one at Quantock. The second was at Ledbury and the third at TW Beach in Hereford which was later transferred to Chivers Hartley, now Premier, at Histon.
- Jams and Condiments: apart from conserves for Sainsbury, most was 'speciality stuff' including products for Burberry's and the Duchess of Devonshire's brand which was made to a recipe approved by the Head Chef at Chatsworth!

When RHM decided that major rationalisation of its entire product portfolio was urgently required, it was originally suggested that the axe should fall on the majority of Ledbury's industrial business. It fell to David Smith to argue successfully that this would be a bad move and that it would be much more effective to close down the speciality retail business, sometimes known as 'Dorset' and eliminate at one hit 200 short-run recipes and a plethora of obscure and complex ingredients and packaging.

acquisition had, in particular, produced one good, and in the long-term for Ledbury Preserves, very important, outcome. In response to the radio interview, RHM's Directors had made a public commitment to keep the Ledbury operations going and to make Ledbury Preserves the centre for their industrial jam business. Thus, within two years, Ledbury became the focal point for a number of acquisitions and integrations. RHM devised a simple strategy for Ledbury Preserves. Their view was that the plant was working far below capacity and so should be 'filled' by acquisition. While it decided not to purchase Samuel Moore Foods from Hazelwoods, it did acquire and integrate three complementary businesses in rapid succession:

- Stewart & Arnold: This was a jam making business already owned by RHM but operating out of a very run down plant in Ashford. Its version of open pan boiling was even more antiquated than Ledbury's in that open copper pans of boiled jam were decanted into mobile stainless steel 'prams' which then had to be trundled across a rutted concrete floor to a point where the contents could be siphoned off via a votator to a holding tank. Operators had to be very skilled to avoid spilling scalding jam onto either the floor or their feet! The extra business was, however, important to Ledbury Preserves as it introduced its first exposure to RHM's Mr Kipling cake business and the capacity to store jam in bulk tanks prior to shipment to customers via road tankers.
- Quantock Preserving Company: This Bridgwater-based business—ironically until 1980, part of Robertson's Food Group—produced private label and retail industrial jams. Again, this was an acquisition of strategic importance rather than simply delivering more volume since it brought with it the ability to supply fresh fruit marmalades to Marks & Spencer and thus consolidated Ledbury's position as the sole M&S preserves supplier, a position which was retained for

the remainder of the company's history. Integration placed huge demands on the Ledbury team as the whole job from stock checking on the day of acquisition through to clearance of the Bridgwater site and commencement of manufacture at Ledbury had to be completed in just four weeks! While that extraordinary timetable was far from ideal, the acquisition also added another string to the industrial bow in that it gave Ledbury the wherewithal to manufacture the filling for Jaffa Cakes, a sophisticated process requiring the ability to supply a material of consistent flavour and texture which, on addition of food acid in a biscuit factory, converts to a gel within 75 seconds. There was so much sensitivity about this product and the process of manufacture that the major Quantock customer would not purchase Jaffa filling from Ledbury until a full year had elapsed. Nonetheless, the team was able within the desperately tight four week time frame, to get the product correctly manufactured and tankered across the North Sea for delivery into the second largest account, a major Belgian biscuit manufacturer!

• Just Juice was acquired from the Irish Dairy Board. The acquisition of this brand, plus associated private label business and plant, more than doubled Ledbury's juice production capacity to over 80 million litres per year.

These changes, alongside similar activity at Droylsden, relating to the acquisition of the Keiller brand and the entirety of the Co-Operative movement's jam manufacturing business, required a huge increase in the number of employees, with the number more than doubling to peak at something in excess of 400. In practice, this very bullish strategy of 'filling up Ledbury' overstretched largely unchanged management resources; it progressively came unstuck and the business nearly imploded under the weight of a vast and complex product portfolio. At the height of this activity, Ledbury Preserves was probably trying to produce:

• 700 industrial recipes
• 200 low volume jam and condiment recipes in the 'Dorset Room'
• 350 retail jam and marmalade recipes
• 100 fruit juice recipes

Recognition that this was unsustainable came at the same time that RHM Foods, of which Ledbury was now a part, commenced a major simplification drive which sought to reduce drastically the numbers of products and customers handled. This programme in the early 1990s has to be set against the background of a challenging period for RHM as its old strategies of cutting the cost fat out of branded operations such as Bisto began to struggle and its profits too began to stagnate. Acquisitions outside the jam arena had been made and to some extent unscrambled, and senior management within the Group were focused on fighting takeover bids such as one from an Australian group, Goodman Fielder Wattie and an anticipated bid from Hanson Trust.

The impact of the simplification programme for Ledbury was substantial. The entire 'Dorset' operation was closed down and trade in private label jams with such customers as Spar, NAAFI and Booker, was discontinued. Recipe rationalisation was used to cull the industrial portfolio to around 250 recipes and 50 customers. A highly experienced RHM factory manager, Philip Buckley, was brought in to manage the consequences and re-impose functional disciplines on what had become a very ragged manufacturing operation. Significantly for the future, he was able to follow up earlier arguments for the retention of the industrial business with a successful proposal that Ledbury Preserves' industrial operations be treated as a profit, rather than a cost, centre. Thus in the mid-nineties a dedicated Ledbury-based industrial business team was set up. By contrast, all other products were sold by RHM personnel working out of offices in either Willesden or Windsor.

'Buns to Guns' and some Schizophrenic Years

It was against this background that in 1992, the industrial conglomerate, Tomkins PLC, acquired RHM in its entirety and was quickly tagged 'the buns to guns' conglomerate as a result of its ownership of businesses as diverse as RHM and Smith & Wesson. Tomkins' ownership brought a key shift in corporate philosophy along the 'small is beautiful' lines. RHM's major divisions were deconstructed into separate profit-responsible businesses; hence Ledbury Preserves became divided into two separate companies:

• The Just Juice Company Limited: This managed all fruit juice production, selling and marketing and was the parent company for the site because, when measured in tonnage, its output was much greater than that of the preserves business.

• James Robertson & Sons Limited: This was an amalgam of Ledbury's preserves operations and the Droylsden manufacturing, marketing and selling activities of the Robertson's and Golden Shred brands. Under this regime, Ledbury had initially Andy Hodson and subsequently Dean Holroyd as its general manager or director.

For the James Robertson operation at Ledbury, a platform for this new era had already been laid via the creation of the industrial business team and the new structure benefited immediately from managed growth in volume, efficiency and profitability of the industrial business. This business stream set out to:

- deliver consistent products;
- provide professional, proactive and highly responsive customer service;
- grow volume and profits via well-targeted new product development in chosen accounts.

It quickly became apparent that this focus and strategy were successfully delivering not only stability but also profitable growth. Tomkins backed the business by supporting expenditure to acquire the majority of the industrial jam and yogfruit business of Stratford Canners, a subsidiary of the now defunct Albert Fisher Group. As it happened, yogfruit itself proved unsuccessful as a result of structural changes which were coincidentally taking place in the dairy industry. However, Tomkins' astute financial management had ensured that most of the costs of acquisition would be paid as a success fee on business gained and retained and thus there was no great penalty for this failure. The upside was that Ledbury gained the capability to pack low sugar products aseptically in bulk, together with scrape-surface processing.

Simultaneously, and sadly, The Just Juice Company's fortunes ran in the opposite direction and eventually the loss of the Ocean Spray franchise prompted the disposal in March 1999 of the entire fruit juice business and the closure of its plant.

7 ⟿ De L'Ora, Just Juice & other Luscious Liquids

Orange What?

If you drank fruit juice in the 1960s, you were probably a rare breed. Of course, everyone knew orange squash but orange juice was a different matter. You might have been old enough to remember your mother getting 'Baby Orange' in a medicine bottle — not something you drank for pleasure but in order to boost your Vitamin C. If your family had been brave enough to go to the pub and not drink beer, you might have drunk a bottle of Britvic Orange — sweetened orange juice often looking dull and tired and sold in a little bottle alongside tonic water. If your family had been really radical, you might occasionally have bought a can of ready to drink Jaffa orange juice or 'Florida Orange,' a concentrated frozen fruit juice imported by Bird's Eye. This one would need a lot of forethought as it had to be thawed and diluted before drinking which hardly encouraged anyone to drink orange juice just because they fancied a glass.

But probably most people had never seen or drunk orange juice. So for Ledbury Preserves, with its traditional and familiar jam range, branching out into the production and sale of fruit juice was a really bold move. Or at least, it was a bold move from a marketing and selling viewpoint whereas in production, fruit juice at first required technology, plant and ingredients which were very familiar. Why? Because making fruit juice was very simple. Unlike jam, no one had to worry about adding pectin and citric acid or combining sugar and glucose with fruit to get a palatable flavour and good consistency. Using orange as the prime example, all that was needed was to take frozen orange juice concentrate, thaw it, dilute it back to its normal strength, pasteurise it and fill it into a glass jar. The challenges were finding a good concentrate to begin with, not burning it during the pasteurisation process and making sure that the bottle was packed in a sterile fashion. And that was how Ledbury Preserves kicked off its fruit juice venture in the late sixties and early seventies.

Somewhere along the line the company came up with the clever idea of packing not only into a square profile, one litre bottle, which was becoming

the staple of the growing European fruit juice business, but also into a much more shapely three-quarter litre jar which had a sloping neck. It is thought that this effective marketing ploy was devised by Ricky Southern; it made the jar easy to handle and meant that it could be sold at an attractive unit price. The very first production line was fairly rudimentary using a semi-automatic filler which handled just sixteen jars per minute. It was soon replaced with a faster machine which quadrupled this output. Before long, this line too became inadequate. It was retained to bottle lower volume and more difficult juices such as pineapple and tomato and a new 200 jars per minute line was installed in 1974, just five years after the first fruit juice sales were recorded.

Despite the fact that fruit juice was so radically different for the consumer, Ledbury Preserves' selling and marketing strategy was essentially a clone of that which had served it well for jam and marmalade. Thus, the offer was primarily to create a private label for the customer with the company's own De L'Ora brand being used as a fall back. Private label was easy to do; the company had good relationships with label printers who could rapidly knock out a label using a standard set of illustrations and so contracts were arranged with many wholesale and cash-and-carry groups in addition to two of the then large multiples, Fine Fare and Tesco. What probably no one had appreciated originally was that the combination of pure fruit juice and the distinctive three-quarter litre bottle was opening up doors that were totally closed to Ledbury Preserves as a jam maker. So, for example, it was possible to sell De L'Ora to greengrocers via fruit markets and to dairies for doorstep delivery. Outlets such as the Co-operative Society—a no-go territory as far as jam was concerned because the organisation had its own preserves plant—became potential customers.

The Pure Fruit Juice Explosion

Another major difference was that, as the seventies progressed, the nation's taste for fruit juice exploded! Jam and marmalade sales in Britain had been in decline for over twenty years because they were seen as dull, old-fashioned and probably not very healthy. On the other hand, slimming diets were becoming popular, people were more interested in healthy eating and Ledbury's fruit juices, which were always produced without sweeteners, additives or preservatives, perfectly fitted the bill. The predominant flavours initially were orange, grapefruit, pineapple and tomato. With one exception, orange was always way out as the number one. The exception came in the mid-seventies when there was a short-lived 'grapefruit diet' craze. At this time, one lady customer wrote to the company asking 'How do I take De L'Ora grapefruit juice so as to slim?' The draft reply suggesting direct injection into her veins was censored by the sales director!

The growth in demand and opportunities for fruit juice also created a great opening for the more imaginative of Ledbury Preserves' sales people. The most notable of these was a Glaswegian sales agent, Ian Hillis, whose territory comprised Scotland in its entirety. Possibly because his accent was so demanding, very few people at Ledbury chose to have long conversations with him and so he was allowed to use his own considerable initiative in developing new sales outlets. Before long, he generated such a high volume of sales that several full trunker loads of De L'Ora made their way up the M6 every Monday morning to his valued customers, including the Scottish Co-ops and the extensive cash-and-carry network which served Scotland's independent stores. In the cash-and-carries, he would ensure that a liberal supply of samples flowed to the truck drivers who cared for the fruit juice aisles and thus would ensure that, while pallets of De L'Ora were easily accessible

WHY DE L'ORA?

The prosaic explanation is that this exotic sounding brandname is just the first three letters of 'Ledbury' in reverse, followed by the first three letters of the word 'orange' in their usual order. All it needed was a couple of capital letters and a judiciously placed apostrophe to transport it far away from its Herefordshire origins!

An alternative is that names like Del Sol and Del Monte, vaguely suggestive of sunshine and tropical beaches, were very much in vogue at this time and so De L'Ora was a simple construct which followed this fashion.

Or, just maybe in the light of Ledbury Preserves' history, it could be a simple adaptation of the brandname Delberry which Avana owned and which had been used by Ledbury's original parent company, D Jones Dickinson, for the cakes that it had sold throughout South Wales until around ten years before the fruit juice business was launched.

at floor level, competitors' products were banished to the upper layers of the racking to gather dust!

The dramatic growth in demand for fruit juice in the Britain of the 1970s meant that many new packaging formats were explored. Various sachets, pouches and tubular containers of dubious integrity were tried but Ledbury Preserves, with considerable foresight, recognised at an early stage the potential offered by the aseptic carton which, at that time, was almost exclusively used for longlife milk. Avana and Ledbury invested in this new technology, forging a relationship with the Swedish company, Tetrapak, which offered a sophisticated carton known as a Tetrabrik. While this pack format is very familiar today, it initially caused great confusion, with consumers unsure whether it contained orange juice or soap powder! For the manufacturing team at Ledbury Preserves, the packing technology was totally unfamiliar. The process of mixing and blending fruit juice remained unchanged but packaging was a whole new world in which the carton was actually formed around a column of flash-pasteurised fruit juice! Micro-biological security depended on packing in an aseptic environment which demanded that the paper of the carton be passed through a bath of hydrogen peroxide and that the final seal be formed through the juice itself. The carton was a sophisticated multi-layer laminate delivered on large reels each containing 2,500 cartons.

Brands, Grand Strategy and International Alliances

Apart from learning new production skills, the introduction of this technology prompted Ledbury Preserves to rethink its sales offering. Reels of Tetrabrik laminate took up a great deal of space and each package was probably ten times more expensive than the label that would be applied to a jar of fruit juice. So it rapidly became apparent that pursuing extensive private label deals would create significant cash flow and storage problems. In addition, it was technically undesirable to switch constantly between cartons that might have been printed months apart; doing so could easily make it difficult to maintain asepticity and any failure of asepticity would be a complete nightmare. Why? Because a carton that had not been absolutely aseptically packed and sealed would allow air to seep in and thus contaminate the juice which would, in turn, ferment, causing the carton to blow up and eventually explode! It is not hard to imagine the chaos and mess in a warehouse if just a few cartons on a pallet on the third tier of a racking system were to start to leak frothing and evil smelling orange juice onto everything below.

For these reasons, a bold but ultimately flawed decision was made in 1980 to focus entirely on the De L'Ora brand and turn down any requests for private label. This strategy was implemented with all seriousness, with even Tesco's private label business being turned down! The other side of the coin was that, for the first time ever, Ledbury Preserves put marketing support behind a brand that it owned. A Bristol-based

HOW DID LEDBURY PRESERVES FIND PEOPLE OF THE RIGHT CALIBRE TO RUN THE SOPHISTICATED TETRABRIK MACHINES?

Here's an interesting example!

You would think that as a special constable in the West Mercia Police, security would have been the role where Allan Clarke started in the jam factory. But the Pozzy often operated in a circuitous way. In 1973, the distribution manager at the jam factory lived in Bosbury, Allan's home village. That's how Allan first found out there was a job going as a chauffeur. He got the job but the need for a chauffeur soon vanished and instead he began driving vans delivering to stores in Herefordshire, Worcestershire, Gloucestershire, Birmingham and Wales.

In 1981, Allan moved to work in the factory. As a Tetrabrik machine operator, he came in at six in the morning to get the machines ready and production started at seven. Blenders would dilute and mix the concentrated juices and then process plant operators would adjust the blend to achieve the correct strength before pasteurising. Allan's role required him to thread the large reel of cartons through a series of rollers and then through a bath of sterilant. Thereafter, the flat reel of cartons passed over the top of the machine and was formed into a tube surrounding the feed of pasteurised fruit juice before a complex set of jaws created and sealed the carton around its contents! This process was fully computer controlled and a long way removed from the semi-craft skills of producing jam and marmalade. Any interruption to the process would require the plants to be shut down and re-sterilised before manufacturing could be resumed.

The shifts ran from six until two and two until ten at night. At 8.30 pm, production stopped to clean the machines down. In later years, a night shift was brought in to clean the machines for the next morning. Production would continue until ten at night, then re-commence at six in the morning.

advertising agency was commissioned to create a local radio campaign for De L'Ora, and then a series of TV adverts. Point of sale material and brochures were generated in cash-and-carries and bottle-collars were developed for use in the dairies. Kate Loxton, technical support technologist at the time when Ledbury Preserves closed, started working at the factory in 1987 and one of her first jobs was on the juice bottle line where she had to put these special offer paper cones on the juice bottles as they went by. As this type of promotion was only run occasionally, there was no machine to do it!

Such intensive activity, coupled with a determined sales drive, propelled De L'Ora to a brand-leading position in the UK fruit juice market, even though the brand was not stocked by all of the multiples. Sadly, this brief moment of euphoria could not be sustained since, almost immediately after this pinnacle had been ascended, the brand stumbled under a double barrelled assault from Del Monte and from aggressive new entrants to the market who were willing to live with the technical and cash-flow problems associated with high paper stocks and therefore offered private label extensively. This onslaught not only rocked the brand but also massively damaged profit margins. Although the strategy of not offering private label was maintained for some time, the fruit juice business lost its pre-eminent position within Avana and eventually, as a rearguard action, a late re-entry into private label had to be undertaken as a defensive measure. Another mid-eighties venture which focused on using the aseptic cartoning technology to create a still, carton-packed, cider under the brand name Trumpet caused considerable interest but was not a lasting commercial success.

Within a few years, ownership by RHM brought about a significant transformation of scale as the Just Juice business was purchased. This not only brought with it the Just Juice brand, which at that time held second place in the UK market, but also significant private label volume, notably with Tesco! There were major manufacturing and engineering implications as the packing machines were due to be brought in to Ledbury from the Just Juice plant in Staffordshire. The space allocated for bottling was reduced and additional bulk juice storage and blending equipment was installed in a new building. In reality, much of the kit was not fit to be moved and a deal was struck with Tetrapak to replace much of the machinery with only modest new expenditure. This major move, happening in parallel with the acquisition of new jam businesses, pushed employment at Ledbury Preserves to its highest level ever, peaking at around 450.

LEDBURY PRESERVES' FOOTBALL CLUB 1984
Back row l-r: Trevor Loader, Paul Trigg, Hughie Boswell, Mick Jones, Pete Febery,
Dave Greening, Terry Fleetwood
Front row l-r: Richard Smith, Melvyn Manns, Tim Green, Steve Bunn, Alan Hale,
Andy Brimmell, Jimmy Loveridge

INTERNATIONAL FOOTBALL SUCCESS

De L'Ora and later Just Juice sponsored a works football team for a number of years. A pitch was built in the field adjacent to the factory and the team started its competitive life in the Herefordshire fourth division.

The first year wasn't great but in the second year the team won its league and was runner up in a cup competition. In the following year, the factory team was again runner up in the league and entered the Frank Peterson Cup. It reached the final of this competition twice.

The next year the side reached its zenith, winning the league and being promoted into the old second division. This was a decent standard of football by any measure. They held their own for twelve months but in the following season came relegation and then relegation again.

During the successful years the football team would go on tour over the Easter weekend. It was one of the first English football sides to travel abroad after the Heysel stadium disaster and received a bit of press coverage as a result. They left on the Friday by bus and stopped over in France. The following day they had a game which was due to be played in Belgium but because of the Heysel tragedy, had to be relocated to Holland. They actually played two games there, one of which was a 1-1 draw and the other a spectacular 11-1 victory. There were also annual football games for charity, jam versus juice, which always attracted a considerable crowd.

OCEAN SPRAY: WHO AND WHAT?

• It all started 75 years ago with three farmers from Massachusetts and New Jersey.

• Hence, Ocean Spray has been around since the 1930s and is a North American agricultural co-operative.

• The business is owned by a large group of cranberry growers throughout North America. As of now, there are about 650 cranberry growers plus 100 Florida grapefruit growers.

• Ocean Spray claims to be the leading producer of canned and bottled juice drinks in North America and has been since 1981. In 2005, they achieved gross sales of roughly $1.4 billion.

• The co-operative has more than 2,000 employees worldwide. Its headquarters are located in Lakeville-Middleboro, Massachusetts, New England.

Shortly before the acquisition of Just Juice, another development took place which was to prove of considerable importance in subsequent years. Ledbury was approached by Ocean Spray, a massive co-operative of cranberry growers in the United States. In Britain up to this time, both cranberries and the Ocean Spray brand were associated almost exclusively with cranberry sauce. The cranberry growers in the United States, however, had seen an opportunity to convert their fruit into a very distinctive drink which, over time, acquired a reputation for delivering significant health benefits. So Ocean Spray wanted to see if they could repeat this success in the UK and, as their business in their home market was very much built around a bottled product, they looked for a packer able to offer good technical skills plus a bottling capability.

Ledbury Preserves met these criteria and so a deal was done to contract pack three varieties of cranberry juice drink into three-quarter litre round bottles. Hence, the factory saw a sudden influx of American visitors ranging from marketing whiz-kids to gruff, feet-on-the-ground, technologists who worked with Ledbury's then juice expert, Duncan McKay, to create products which would suit the UK palate. This required the blending of cranberry and other fruit juice concentrates with sweeteners and natural flavours, because cranberry juice alone would be far too harsh to drink. At this stage, Ledbury Preserves was simply responsible for manufacturing while a High Wycombe based food broker handled sales, advertising and distribution. Brits were, at first, slow to appreciate the delights of the cranberry but gradually the advertising programme and favourable press comments eroded this initial reluctance and volumes began to move ahead. By the early nineties, volume growth and mainstream positioning dictated a move into carton packaging, and with that the brand really took off. It became a mainstay of the fruit juice business, not only because it generated substantial volumes, but also because the pricing structure agreed at the outset paid Ledbury a consistent manufacturing fee and meant that margins were not subject to erosion when raw material costs rose.

In the fullness of time, when in 1993 the Just Juice Company became a separate entity within RHM in the Tomkins regime, the management of the new company was able successfully to make a case to the Directors of Ocean Spray Cranberries Inc that The Just Juice Company should take on the full responsibility of the brand and so all the marketing, selling and distribution activities were transferred into Ledbury, firstly under managing director Brian Metcalfe and from 1995, under Ginny Knox.

The growth of Ocean Spray was seemingly unstoppable. For several years, it grew at over forty per cent per annum, fuelled by its ability to cure cystitis in the old and its use in fashionable cocktails for the young! It became the UK's number one 'juice drink,' (a definition which excludes pure juices) and the UK became far and away the most important market for Ocean Spray cranberries outside North America. It also became the largest, most profitable and most exciting part of Just Juice's portfolio.

Back to Just Jam!

Sadly, however, this success was also to lead to the ultimate demise of fruit juice manufacturing in Ledbury. In 1997, Ocean Spray's new international president, Malcolm Lloyd, decided strategically that Ocean Spray should link itself with the largest juice manufacturer in the UK, which was Gerber. He gave notice to withdraw from the business with Just Juice/RHM. Ginny Knox, Just Juice's MD and Paul Wilkinson, RHM's chairman, flew straight to New England to argue, cajole and attempt to persuade the cranberry co-operative to change their collective minds. However, it was impossible and the business was lost.

The Juice business was now in a very difficult position. Without Ocean Spray, it had a huge amount of excess capacity and it was making a loss. There were two urgent imperatives: to increase volume and to cut costs and there was very little time to play with! The management team pulled together and through a combination of creativity and hard work, managed to replace the Ocean Spray volume within six months. The first big win was a large chunk of Sainsbury's own label business, followed by a number of contract manufacturing wins and also the launch of a number of branded, Just Juice initiatives. These included the expansion of the innovative

The 'new' processing plant for fruit juices. Ocean Spray drinks were originally bottled on this line.

Here is a typical Ocean Spray recipe for a homemade drink incorporating their Cranberry Juice Cocktail. It illustrates both the versatility of the product and its close connection with perceptions of health. The drink is called CRANBERRY BURST.

INGREDIENTS:

6 ounces Ocean Spray® Cranberry Juice Cocktail with Calcium
2 ounces orange juice
2 ounces ginger ale or diet ginger ale
Orange slice, garnish

DIRECTIONS:

Pour all ingredients, except garnish, into a glass with ice. Garnish with orange slice.

Makes 1 serving.

PER SERVING; Cal. 160 (7% DV), Fat Cal. 0, Pro 0g (0% DV), Carb. 40g (13% DV), Fat 0g (0% DV), Chol. 0mg (0%DV), Sod. 30mg (1% DV), Vit. A 104RE (10% DV), Vit. C 84mg (139% DV), Vit. E 1mg (3%DV), Calcium 79 mg (7%DV), Iron 0mg (1% DV), Folate 17Ug (4%DV), Zinc 0mg (0%DV), Pot. 149mg (4% DV), Dietary Exchange: Fruit: 2.5

(Accessed from www.oceanspray.com on 21 February 2008)

half-litre PET bottle range, the launch of the first range of gable-topped one litre long-life cartons (containing a mix of concentrated juice and juice not from concentrate) and Just Juice's own range of cranberry juice drinks.

This was a fantastic achievement but unfortunately this mix of products was not as profitable as the Ocean Spray products they had replaced. Cost-cutting was essential to make up the difference and so the factory team under David Holmes, the operations director, worked with a team of consultants to calculate what could be saved. In the end, the answer was about one million pounds a year!

So had the business been rescued? It seemed so for a while. However, the market for pure juices was by that time a world market and events in other parts of Europe could have a dramatic impact in the UK. The German juice packers are the largest in Europe and throughout the early and middle part of the nineties, they had been rapidly expanding to service the emerging markets in Eastern Europe. However, in the late nineties, the Russian economy collapsed and the German manufacturers had to find new markets for their products. Britain looked attractive and large amounts of cheap juice started to be dumped here. The Just Juice Company was simply too small to be able to access the economies of scale of the Germans and the Just Juice and De L'Ora brands were not strong enough to be able to retain a premium price.

Finally and sadly, the company had to admit defeat and Tomkins put it up for sale. In 1998, the brands and some of the plant were sold to Del Monte based in Kings Lynn, Norfolk and after thirty years, fruit juice manufacture at Ledbury ceased. A total of 185 jobs were lost, with just a couple of employees transferring to Norfolk and a handful transferring to work for James Robertson & Sons on the Ledbury site. The buildings remained and the management of the preserves business now had the task of maintaining them and looking for new ways of putting them to use.

8 ⟶ Marks & Spencer:
Major Customer and Major Influence

M&S and Ledbury Preserves: Some History

Ledbury Preserves were definitely suppliers of jams to M&S by the late 1930s. According to a checking list dating from 1939, Ledbury Preserves were then supplying five jams into M&S under the brand name 'Malvern' which M&S believe was used at that time exclusively for their business. The jams were supplied direct to individual stores which were able to order as they chose provided they could make up an order for not less than 144 jars! Jars were packed in boxes of 24 and were delivered within two weeks after the order had been placed. The range supplied appears to have excluded any marmalades but the jam varieties, if not the prices, sound very familiar!

- 1lb jars: Strawberry, Raspberry and Apricot—sold at 6d (2.5p) each
- 2lb jars: Strawberry and Raspberry—sold at 10½d (4.5p) each

Although little is known now about the early years of the relationship, oral histories suggest that the supply continued through the war years. There may have been an interruption at some stage because it is understood that, as related in Chapter 4, Sir Julian Hodge personally intervened not long after Avana had acquired the company to help re-establish the relationship. During the late 1950s and early 1960s the company supplied a full range of preserves: jams, marmalades and mincemeat, although this was probably not on an exclusive basis.

At some stage during the mid or late 1960s, the supply of most of the M&S marmalade was lost to Quantock Preserving Co, although Ledbury continued to produce one very dark and bitter marmalade product which was the personal favourite of Lord Sieff. The Bridgwater-based Quantock business, which was later to become part of the Robertson's Foods Group, was a significant competitor to Ledbury in both retail and industrial preserves. Quantock presented to M&S the attractive concept of making Seville orange marmalade in season from fresh fruit. Ledbury at that time made its marmalades in the traditional manner from oranges that were pre-processed and held in brine to permit year-round manufacture. It lacked the facilities and possibly the will to undertake once a year manufacture from fresh fruit, which additionally required both accurate estimating of demand and the financial commitment to store a full twelve months' stock. Nevertheless, the supply of jams, by this stage on an exclusive basis, continued to grow as M&S extended its reach as a significant national food retailer.

By the 1980s, Ledbury Preserves accounted for only a small part of the total business which the Avana group conducted with M&S and the relationship was further underpinned when Northern Foods, the largest M&S food supplier, became a major shareholder in Avana Group. Avana's chairman, Dr John Randall, had strong personal ties with the senior management at the Marks & Spencer Head Office in Baker Street, built on a record of consistent supply of high quality products and first rate new product development, particularly with cakes and ready meals. At the same time Randall took steps to ensure that the business didn't become over-dependent on any one customer, and the growth of the Avana Group during the 1980s was supported by a number of acquisitions of companies which had little or no relationship with M&S. Randall also stood his ground with M&S when he felt it necessary, once refusing to agree to an M&S request to its suppliers to provide financial support to an Israeli initiative involving the controversial figure of Menachem Begin. Another example concerned a complaint of mouldy jam made during a visit to Japan by Lord Rayner, then the M&S chairman. Although the complaint was spurious, Rayner agreed to provide financial compensation and on his return directed his minions to recover this from the supplier. Randall repeatedly refused and eventually the M&S staff had to find a way of disguising their internal reporting to avoid having to tell the chairman of their failure.

In the mid 1980s, Ledbury Preserves started to adopt a more proactive approach to the M&S catalogue, which had remained largely unchanged for many years. An initial innovation, surprisingly enough, was the launch of raspberry jam to supplement a jam range which featured only strawberry, blackcurrant, apricot and, from time to time, black cherry. Following this successful introduction, a significant further step was made by introducing a fresh grapefruit marmalade. For Ledbury Preserves, apart from providing additional sales, this had two great advantages:

• A significant erosion of Quantock's twenty-year stranglehold on M&S marmalade.
• Because fresh grapefruit could be sourced largely throughout the year, the financial and forecasting demands were that much less onerous than for Seville orange marmalade.

This development, coupled with packaging innovation, proved to be of great importance when, in 1987, it became apparent that the owners of the Quantock business were in a mood to sell. Hence, when Ledbury Preserves, under RHM's ownership, was able to purchase Quantock's assets and business, the move was welcomed by M&S and from that time onwards, Ledbury Preserves resumed the role of solus preserves supplier. During the 1990s the range was developed to include, once again, low sugar jams and 'spreads' in which concentrated fruit juices replaced sugar as the sweetener. Another important development was the expansion of seasonal products beyond mincemeat to include luxury preserves such as Apricot Conserve with Amaretto and other indulgent and unusual variations designed as gifts. One of the most notable of these was a tall jar containing an exceptional marmalade made with Seville oranges, sweet oranges and cranberries; this was marketed with a long-handled jam-spoon attached.

The quality of products supplied to M&S was always a particular feature and over the years, improvements were made to operating systems, machinery and ingredients to maintain high standards. The fresh fruit marmalades made on the 'High Level' boiling plant using ingredients prepared on the citrus processing plant in the Fruit Preparation department, and the conserves made on the E Section vacuum boiling pans, have repeatedly been chosen as 'best in class' by connoisseurs and consumers alike. There are jams and marmalades for sale at higher prices with exclusive brand names in supermarkets, West End stores and specialist retailers, but very few can consistently match the standard of product routinely produced at Ledbury for M&S. Premier Foods, who know a lot about making jam, implicitly acknowledged this when they decided to relocate all the relevant production equipment from Ledbury to Histon rather than attempt to match any of the products on their existing machinery.

An additional and important implication of the supply of retail preserves was that Ledbury had an almost automatic inroad into companies supplying M&S with finished products that might incorporate jam or mincemeat. Most notably, these were bakers of cakes and other bakery goods but they eventually also included suppliers of savoury dishes and sandwiches where a jam or jelly might be used either as an accompaniment or an ingredient. In the 1960s and 1970s M&S initiated a process to 'approve' formally an ingredient such as jam for use by a bakery supplier; hence a widely used raspberry jam was commonly known as RM156. This designation simply meant that it was the one hundred-and-fifty-sixth ingredient to be approved for use in bakeries. In later years, the volume of products sold as ingredients for inclusion in M&S products, including large quantities of mincemeat as well as jam and other ingredients, actually exceeded the volume of their retail preserves.

What Was It Like To Be a Marks & Spencer Supplier?

One of the first things to note is that the mind-set required to be an M&S supplier was very much part of the Avana Group culture rather than being purely a Ledbury Preserves phenomenon. In fact, supplying M&S was infinitely more important to Avana Bakeries and R F Brookes than it was to Ledbury since both of these companies were virtually dedicated M&S suppliers. At Ledbury, from the 1950s forward, the proportion of turnover accounted for by M&S ranged between ten and twenty per cent. So while it was important, it did not dominate and other customers' requirements were not routinely sacrificed to M&S. Nonetheless, simply being a supplier to Marks & Spencer exerted a crucial influence on many of Ledbury Preserves' disciplines; thus, for example, hygiene inspections frequently included the fruit juice plant even though the company never succeeded in supplying juices to M&S.

To many employees, most aspects of working with M&S were shrouded in mystery and only a handful of individuals were permitted the privilege of face to face contact with visiting executives. It is now astonishing to think that until 1985, the rigours of managing the M&S account were considered to be far too substantial for the sales director or his team to have any involvement whatsoever! In the early 1970s, there was a two-tiered commercial approach to the account, with the managing director taking the overview while a designated executive was responsible for day to day management. The latter was something of a loner who quite possibly inherited the mantle of caring for M&S because he appeared to be the only person in the business capable of preparing a product costing. Most visits however—and they could be very frequent and demanded many days of preparation and window dressing—had a distinct factory focus and were led by either food technologists or hygiene managers. The food technologist role presented an interesting irony. Preserves were undoubtedly one of the 'safer' foods in comparison, for example, with chilled savoury dishes or canned fish where the food safety challenge was much more high profile. Hence, new technologists would often be sent to Ledbury to learn the ropes and the members of Ledbury's technical management would invest many hours training them in the specifics of preserves and the more general aspects of quality control and food hygiene. Once this introductory phase had been completed, roles would be reversed and the now very powerful, influential, young and sometimes glamorous technologists would come into Ledbury like gods, dispensing directives and instructions and wielding the feared power of veto which could consign an entire production run, if considered less than perfect, to perdition.

It is also worth reflecting on the fact that new product developers were a very important part of the M&S relationship. M&S had its own development team which would present new product or packaging concepts for a supplier such as Ledbury to consider. Ledbury, too, had its own dedicated team responsible for product development although this role was essentially one of recipe development only; packaging was neither its brief nor expertise. At a time when most retailers' own brands were simply standard jams or marmalades differentiated solely by different labels, this ability to create and develop new products was key to both the direct M&S relationship and the indirect relationship with their bakery suppliers.

Thus, although the sales team was for many years specifically excluded from even speaking to M&S, for other functions the customer/supplier relationship extended across a wide range of the disciplines within the business. This was in complete contrast with the relationship with a mainstream grocery customer such as Tesco or Spar where almost every aspect was entirely managed by the sales director alone. As a result of the unique complexity of the relationship, it was actually very difficult for new suppliers to become approved by M&S and this acted as something of a safeguard and protection for Ledbury Preserves. This was notably evident when a Dutch supplier made significant initial steps towards persuading M&S to purchase from them a range of reduced sugar jams. While the products themselves had impressed, they never made it to the shelves because the intended supplier simply proved incapable of coping with the intensity, detail and rigour of the multi-functional relationship that M&S expected. Similar considerations would come into play when Premier later faced the task of transferring the Ledbury production into their own factory at Histon.

Major Gain or Major Pain?

Over the past 30 years, the number of plants producing jams and marmalades in the UK has fallen from over twenty to a mere handful. This inevitably prompts the question: Was it the M&S relationship which enabled Ledbury

Preserves to survive for so long? The answer is probably that, while it was not the only factor, it was one of four or five major contributors to the business' longevity. So what did M&S bring to the party that was new and distinctive?

• A consistent and, certainly from the 1960s to the 1980s, unique focus on outstanding eating qualities and more recently, on the provenance of the ingredients used. The fact that the M&S consumer was willing to pay appropriately for products using outstanding ingredients enabled Ledbury to run a distinctive retail and industrial product portfolio that was, at least to some extent, distanced from the pricing pressures associated with the virtually commoditised products found elsewhere in the preserves market.

• M&S exerted a consistent pressure to improve manufacturing processes and to invest in the plant. While it could sometimes appear that their standards were inconsistent, the effect was that the Ledbury factory was always cleaner and more disciplined than many of its competitors, even though the buildings and the kit may have been ageing. This became very apparent around 1988 when a number of competing preserves businesses came on to the market. Ledbury executives visiting these plants frequently encountered practices that would never have been countenanced in Little Marcle Road! For example, Samuel Moore Foods, mentioned in Chapter 6 as a possible but rejected acquisition, had its jam boiling area at the rear of its factory which itself was located half way down an incline. The boiling facility was separated from the outside world simply by a curtain of heavy duty plastic slats and, at ground level, a six-inch-high bund. When it rained, muddy water from the surrounding fields flowed with little let or hindrance into the crucial boiling area! Such poverty of control would have been totally unacceptable in a supplier to M&S.

• Preserves were never going to be the focus of intensive innovation in the way that recipe dishes, sandwiches or even cakes were. Nonetheless, the M&S expectation of regularly being able to present something new to a dedicated and adventurous clientele placed an emphasis on pro-activity which was beneficial to Ledbury Preserves and gave it further differentiation from its competitors. The desire to innovate included packaging as well as product and so it was that in 1986, the management of Ledbury and M&S jointly recognised that the familiar and predictable straight-sided jars in use at the time were not doing full justice to the excellence of the jams and marmalades that they contained. Therefore a comprehensive programme was put in place to create a bespoke tapered and faceted jar which, while challenging at the time of its introduction, generated an increase of approaching twenty per cent in sales in a dull market place and gave Ledbury Preserves considerable kudos with the bright, young marketeers of RHM when the business was acquired in 1987.

• Last but not least, the M&S relationship ensured that there was linkage between the retail and industrial portfolios whereas elsewhere these were kept well apart. This linkage was one of the factors that enabled later Ledbury Preserves management to recognise and capitalise upon the potential to create very high quality, performance-specific industrial preserves that would command a premium price.

Filling 15 cwt tanks of jams for bakery use

9 ✤ Buckets, Boxes and Big Tanks

Cheap, Red and Easy?

'It's cheap and it's red and it's easy.' That was a common view of jams made for bakers rather than packed into jars. In fact, nothing could be further from the truth. Industrial jam, as it has been commonly called in the last two decades is, in many ways, much more complex to manufacture and control than retail preserves. Industrial products are supplied to very demanding customers, often at short notice and they have to perform in a cake or a biscuit as precisely and consistently as a chip must in a computer or a fuel-injector in a car.

To illustrate that idea, listen to the observations of Mark Phelan, Ledbury Preserves' manufacturing manager from late 2007 and formerly engineering manager in a major UK biscuit plant:

'When I first started as a project engineer in a biscuit factory, I thought jam came in jars and was spread with a knife; I certainly hadn't appreciated the complex demands put on the humble filling of Jaffa Cakes and Jam Sandwich biscuits. I, like most people, gave the rheology of the jam very little attention while consuming the biscuits. However, coming from university with a degree in Chemical Engineering and discovering that my first practical encounter with a non-Newtonian fluid was to be something I had eaten on many occasions without giving it a lot of thought, was quite a revelation.'

So what does the jam in a jam sandwich biscuit have to do?
• Typically, it arrives on site in a twenty-tonne tanker and after various quality checks, it is put into storage tanks, from which it is pumped possibly as much as 100 metres across the factory to a small holding vessel.
• From this vessel, the jam is re-circulated by a positive displacement pump through a twenty-four nozzle depositor head, each nozzle releasing a precise quantity of jam onto the biscuit as it passes underneath. If it deposits too much jam, it spills out of the edge of the biscuit—very messy! If there is too little, you have a disappointed customer—equally unsatisfactory!
• The jam also acts as an edible and delicious glue, keeping the two halves of the biscuit together. However, while they must not separate, the top and bottom must be able to slide over each other to allow the plant's 'picking

fingers' to re-align any mis-capped biscuits. If this did not happen, the biscuits would not fit into their packet and would cause major plant downtime at the wrapping machines.

• Equally, the flow properties of the jam are important because it has to flow at the point of deposit, but not so freely that it will run straight out of the biscuit. Thus, anyone who has ever eaten a really good 'jammy' biscuit knows about the unique 'chewy' jam that is its trademark. It has to look good too, with a deep natural colour—which it must keep throughout its long shelf-life—and a domed rather than a limp appearance!

In summary, the jam needs to withstand numerous pumping operations, flow well enough at temperature to deposit, but not run off the biscuit, partially set at reduced temperature to act as a glue to hold the biscuits together, but not set so firm that the biscuit top and bottom cannot slide over each other. Finally, it has to deliver that unique texture and lest we forget, it must taste really good when the packet is opened. So, clearly there is rather more to jam than that jar tucked away in the kitchen cupboard!!'

Such challenging demands are not only found in jams destined for biscuits so consider some examples of what the jam might have to do when used in a cake:

• A jam layered into a Swiss roll will need to be absolutely smooth and capable of being spread evenly through an eight inch wide 'fishtail' depositor. Although the deposit will be thin, it must retain its colour and deliver a flavour that is sufficiently distinctive to be clearly tasted within the sponge roll and probably also through a layer of butter cream.

• The jam used in a 'slice', such as a Bakewell or Victoria slice, also needs to deliver good flavour but in this case, it will need to be deposited onto a sponge batter before it is baked but still retain its shape, position and flavour despite being baked for nearly twenty minutes at up to 170° centigrade! That calls for skilled use of at least two types of fruit pectin and possibly gums to achieve the right degree of stability.

As we have seen, when attention is switched from cakes to biscuits, an understanding of differential flow viscosities and the science of 'sheering' becomes essential. The jam used in a well known and brand-leading 'jammy' biscuit has to be engineered to a very high level to enable it to be pumped over long distances and stored in bulk. Once boiled and cooled, it has first to be pumped into a storage tank at the jam factory and from there, into a road tanker which will deliver it to the biscuit plant where it has to perform exactly as Mark Phelan has described. But perhaps the most exciting and originally scary of the applications is the filling for Jaffa Cakes. Chapter 6 has already outlined the high customer expectations associated with this unique material and many Ledbury Preserves' personnel have genuinely had nightmares

about getting its manufacture and delivery right! Jaffa is delivered to the customer as a dense syrup to which food acid is added to enable the filling to set in no more than sixty seconds before the Jaffa Cake is topped off with chocolate. But the filling must set perfectly, not as rubbery as a jelly-baby but nor can it be soft and sloppy. As with the previous examples mentioned, it must have a characteristic and consistent flavour and this demands that the oils, fruit juices or flavours used in it, in very tiny proportions, must be evenly distributed before the product leaves the factory.

Persistence, Pain and Profit

It will thus be seen that a wide range of skills and scientific understanding is required to supply industrial jams. That understanding needs to encompass both the manufacture in Ledbury and all the subtle nuances of usage in a biscuit factory, bakery or maybe a frozen food plant. As the customers for these products have become larger and more sophisticated, the demands on suppliers have become ever greater. Therefore, Ledbury Preserves had to develop and change in order to develop a market leading role for itself in this challenging sector.

What stages of development of this unusual business can we identify?

• From 1928 to the time of World War II, industrial or—as they were then known—confectionery jams, were probably Ledbury Preserves' biggest sellers. Old photographs show Ledbury Preserves' lorries bearing the logo 'Confectionery Jam Specialists.' With many housewives at the time making their own jam at home, it seems logical to recognise that the biggest customers at this time would have been bakers and these were probably supplied via specialist wholesalers. Clearly D Jones Dickinson, Ledbury Preserves' parent company for a quarter of a century until the mid 1950s, was itself a major customer as it used a wide range of jams for the small cakes produced in its Dowlais bakery.

• The 1950s through to the 1970s saw some significant technical innovations. As has already been noted, Ledbury Preserves claimed to have been the first UK manufacturer to develop continuous evaporation as a manufacturing process and to introduce the use of mobile returnable tanks for deliveries. At the same time, however, the company's natural market place was shrinking as three large bakery conglomerates, Associated British Foods, Ranks Hovis McDougall and Spillers-French, bought up local bakers and assumed dominant market positions in the supply of bread and cakes. As the first two of these companies possessed in-house jam manufacturing, Ledbury Preserves' scope was progressively more and more restricted. Attempts were therefore made to diversify into other sectors and the most notable of these came in the early 1970s, with initially successful moves to supply fruit preparations for yoghurt and other desserts. For as long as the dairy industry accepted products that were either canned or contained preservative, Ledbury Preserves did well. But as the market became more sophisticated and demanded larger containers of preservative-free fillings, Ledbury—lacking the requisite technology—lost ground and eventually withdrew from this sector for almost twenty years.

• Thus, during the late seventies and the majority of the eighties, the approach to industrial preserves could probably be accurately described as benign neglect. Existing jam business was largely retained but industrial jam was very much an 'also-ran', lagging well behind the booming fruit juice business and a retail preserves business which continued to offer opportunities for growth and development, especially as interest in premium products began to burgeon.

• This all changed during the first years of ownership by RHM. While RHM did not insist that Ledbury supplied all of the jam required by its Manor Bakeries subsidiary, it did strive massively to increase Ledbury's output by integrating first its own Stewart & Arnold business and then the industrial preserves output of the Quantock Preserving Company which was acquired. It was, however, at this point that the misconception of industrial preserves as 'cheap, red and easy' threatened to undermine the drive for growth. Ledbury Preserves was now trying to supply the largest and most demanding customers and simultaneously bring together three separate product portfolios. There was initially a failure to understand the high level of skill that had become essential and so a business sector that should have rapidly grown its output from 1,500 tonnes per year to over 10,000 tonnes per year, got only a little beyond half way towards that goal. The causes were nearly always a failure to maintain product consistency or an inability to deliver on time. It would have been very easy at this stage for the industrial business to have closed because its reputation was poor and its profitability negative. There were, however, members of the management team who perceived that a greater level of focus and a realistic assignment of overhead costs could deliver a very different result. They persuaded RHM to try a different approach.

• Hence, from 1993 onwards, industrial preserves was treated as a separate profit centre and it evolved its own philosophy of winning business by doing everything well, developing new products both reactively and proactively and progressively bolting on complementary skills and capacity. A platform for this had to be established by rationalising the range down from 500 to 250 products to reduce complexity and by reducing the number of customers to around fifty whose existing or potential volume would justify a high level of sales input and customer service. A distinctively personal view of the rigours inherent in the process of creating and launching new industrial products is presented by Dominic Shaw on the following page. Dominic had hands-on experience of both the technical and the commercial aspects of this approach.

JUST NOT CRICKET
Dominic Shaw

Ledbury Preserves prided itself on its detailed knowledge of 'live' pectin chemistry. We made things work in the factory despite the fact that there were more variables than you could shake a stick at: pH, TSS, temperature, tea breaks, orders for volumes we should have made on the pilot plant, sales forecasts that were as likely to be achieved as Hereford United were to win the Champion's League, the product development team's recipe accuracy, Steve Bunn's definition of 'fresh', Denzil's interpretation of accurate weight control at High Level, Melvyn's take on what 'out of specification' meant—I could go on. Looking back over the nine years I spent in technical management at Ledbury, our logical and painstaking approach to one particular development brief fills me with a real sense of pride. 'Which one?' I hear you ask. 'Was it "find another strawberry variety for M&S" trial number twenty-two? Was it "stop the Mandarin Marmalade floating" trial fifteen? The fourth complete reduced-sugar jam range for M&S? Dessert Sauces? Christmas 1994, 1995 or 1997? Liquorice spread? Tomato and Garlic jam? The ninth 'let's get the black bits out of Jaffa by using citrus pectin rather than sulphited apple' trial? The 'prove we can fill a 62 per cent TSS industrial jam without it growing its own fur coat within a week' trials? Turkish Delight? Vanilla Thriller?

While these were all achievements of which we could be justly proud, for me our crowning glory was our contribution to Cherry Valley's Duck a L'Orange for M&S, a product so simple in concept yet so fiendishly complex in execution . . . It was simple: you took a raw duck breast, you covered it in M&S bitter orange marmalade and you sold it for massively more than the cost of the components . . . brilliant. It was fiendishly complex: 'Hold on, the marmalade keeps falling off . . . make it thicker please!' and so we did, four or five times, I seem to recall. We gave up trying to cold fill it at about trial three and gave up hot filling and repumping at trial four, when Mac gave me a bill for a new pump. Trial five used a Silverson mixer to make a very thick orange mousse, but M&S thought the absence of long pieces of shred (well, any pieces, to be honest!) rather compromised the product quality. We went back to the drawing board. Trial six used glucose syrup: 'Why is the ingredient list different to what's on a jar of Medium Cut?' 'Ooops! Trial seven: agar. Trial eight: carageenan. Trial nine: starch. Trial ten: guar. Trials eleven through nineteen: combinations of all of the foregoing. Trials twenty through twenty-four: higher solids. Trials twenty-five through thirty: lower solids (it's all down to water migration, you see). Two weeks to launch and we'd still got a product that ate fantastically well but needed to have the shreds stuck on with drawing pins. We thought outside the box: 'Could we supply a packet of sauce with the raw duck?' 'Could they lay the shreds across the meat?' 'Poke the ends of the shreds into small holes stabbed into the breast?' 'What about . . . ?' 'Have you considered . . . ?' 'I've got it! Oh, maybe not.' I forgot who came up with the answer—probably one of the Cherry Valley team. They ended up putting two breasts into each tray . . . there was nowhere for the marmalade to go, you see! Despite the fact that our technical know-how couldn't solve the problem, I was and remained immensely proud of our efforts. I was even more proud of our collective restraint when we were told the product was being de-listed six weeks later . . . !!!

So, not everything that was tried delivered total success. Nonetheless, the combination of a cogent strategy, persistence in innovation and attention to detail laid the basis for a period of steady growth that built the output of the industrial business over a period of fourteen years from 7,000 tonnes per year to virtually double that figure. Along the way, various additions to the portfolio were trialled. Another venture into yogfruit came close to success and succeeded in providing the company with the ability to create and sell low sugar, preservative-free products; in due course, this led to a venture to supply sauces to the ice cream industry. Specialised plant was purchased to process chocolate and toffee products so that Ledbury Preserves could become more of a 'one stop shop' for sweet products. A very successful initiative saw the creation of a business in industrial mincemeat which, from small beginnings using a somewhat Heath Robinson assemblage of kit, grew to supply over 2,000 tonnes per year to specialist mince pie producers throughout and beyond the UK.

At its peak, customers for the industrial business included cake bakers of all shapes and sizes, bakers of doughnuts, buns and other morning goods, frozen and chilled food manufacturers, poultry processors, sandwich makers and dessert specialists. It has always been difficult to define and quantify this diverse market place but it is generally recognised that, in a market that was rarely better than flat, Ledbury Preserves had consistently grown volumes to a point where it was supplying around one third of all of the industrial preserves used in Britain. Measured in tonnage, industrial preserves had thus risen from being the 'also-ran' to represent no less than sixty per cent of Ledbury Preserves' manufacturing output and an equally significant proportion of its profits.

Dave Jones is a rugged boulder of a man who used to compete in tug of war for Wales. In 1989, he was pulled into the jam factory to begin work on the retail palletiser in D Section. He soon became a leading hand and then a chargehand

In the early 1990s, the factory was losing money and drastic action was taken. Shift work stopped; redundancies were made. Dave went back on the line. The factory started at 6am and ran continuously until closing. It was hard work but something positive came out of the experience. Product was more consistent because of fewer shift changes. This lesson was to be important to Dave when he moved into the manufacturing of industrial jams.

Next, however, Dave was given a short-term project on a jobbing line for a Marks & Spencer promotion. When the project finished, Dave thought he would be out on the streets but the factory wasn't finished with him yet! He was asked to become a chargehand on the industrial section.

There had never been chargehands in this sector before, just the manager to oversee operations. Dave was thrown in at the deep end. At this time, the manufacture of industrial jams was spread throughout the factory, with kit in every nook and cranny and even upstairs. Dave cross-trained his staff to work at different stations and introduced structure to combat the 'slap happy' work method (or lack of method) that existed.

Business flourished; at the start, industrial jam demand was a few thousand tonnes a year. Things took off in a big way. From 1991 onwards, a thousand tonnes were gained most years, with the jam factory cranking out a whopping seventeen thousand tonnes of industrial jam in 2007, its last full year of production.

10 ⤙ How Ledbury Became the Nation's Suet Capital

An Opportunity Arises

The closure of the juice operation had left the preserves business occupying a large site with considerable overheads and the Managing Director, Dean Holroyd, knew that the best way to address this legacy would be to bring in a substantial piece of new business to Ledbury. An ideal opportunity presented itself in 2000 when RHM's Centura Foods division started drawing up plans to close its factory in Greatham in County Durham, where Sharwoods sauces and Atora suet were manufactured. The manufacturing Manager at Ledbury at the time, Chris Joules, had had previous experience with the suet operation and together, Holroyd and he lobbied hard and successfully for it to be transferred to Ledbury and located in the old juice building. At the same time, the sauce production was relocated to Droylsden. The plan was announced in 2001 and the relocation was completed in the summer of 2002.

Much of the suet processing and packaging machinery from Greatham was retained but considerable costs were associated with the refurbishment of the buildings and uplifting and relocating the equipment, as well as purchasing and installing a good deal of ancillary equipment, amounting in total to over £1.3m. When the project was completed, in time and on budget, the new factory was a virtual showpiece in comparison with the neighbour-

ing preserves production units. The generous floor area of the old juice building had enabled an optimal layout of equipment and offices and the building had been properly refurbished to meet modern day food factory standards.

The first manager of the Suet department in Ledbury, David Ruminski, had been hardened by many years of setting up and running factories in China. He gathered a team around him, made up of a core of people with experience in the preserves business and others new to the business, and quickly this team formed its own identity and esprit de corps. Having said that, old habits died hard and the habit of jam boilers to hose everything down with water spread to the suet factory, causing repeated difficulties for the effluent plant operators to deal with.

The factory had a noticeably different feel compared with the preserves manufacturing buildings. It was kept cool by air conditioning whereas

MEDICAL EVIDENCE

Dr. W. B. Vaile, M.R.C.S., Medical Officer in charge of a Sanatorium, gives some striking testimony to the value of Beef Suet in a paper contributed to *The Lancet*.

"For six years in every home where I have had a case of pulmonary tuberculosis (consumption) I have strongly advised the mother to insist upon everyone eating fat, *and to give them liberal and frequent suet. I have no failures to record.* In no home where this has been done have any further cases been brought to my notice."

Dr. Saleeby (Chairman of the National Birth Rate Commission) writes in similar strain :

"The young human being requires a continous supply of this substance (the Vitamin A in Beef Suet) for normal development from its real beginning nine months before birth until the 18th year. . . . But further we learn that this Fat Soluble A helps to protect the body against infection, very notably by tuberculosis." (Fat Soluble A is the A Vitamin.) Note the remark " nine months before birth."

In other words, " ATORA " is as essential to the mother as to the child. It should be included regularly in the diet, in dumplings and puddings, and also taken directly in milk, milk puddings, and porridge.

the preserves building was hot, sometimes almost unbearably so in summer, and it had a different smell. To prevent the risks of fat being carried around the site on people's shoes, a separate shoe changing regime was soon introduced and all this contributed

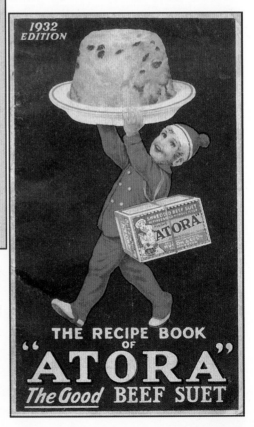

to a perception that the Atora department was a business within a business. Management did nothing to dispel this perception and it arguably contributed to the eventual decision to leave suet production in Ledbury following closure of the preserves factory and the sale of the site.

Building on the Atora heritage

Atora suet had originally been launched in the late nineteenth century by Gabriel Hugon, a Frenchman working in Manchester. Traditional beef suet, rendered from the hard fat found around the kidneys of cattle, was only available from butchers and needed to be kept cool prior to use. Hugon developed a process of stabilising suet by melting the hard fat, allowing it to recrystal-

---

SECTION IX

Sundries

In addition to using "ATORA" in the recipes in this book, keep a packet handy, for you will find it useful in so many other dishes. For example:—

MILK PUDDINGS

Always add a tablespoon "ATORA" to each pint of milk when making rice, semolina, tapioca, sago or ground rice puddings. Immediately, you will notice the difference for the pudding will be richer looking, more creamy in flavour. Whether you bake the milk pudding slowly in the oven or cook it in a double saucepan or pressure cooker don't forget the tablespoon of "ATORA" to each pint.

PORRIDGE

For porridge made with oatmeal or other prepared oats, add a teaspoon "ATORA" for each person. This gives a marked improvement in flavour.

BASTING

"ATORA" is excellent for basting. Sprinkle on the joint, fowl, etc., as required.

PANCAKES OR YORKSHIRE PUDDING BATTER

Having made the batter for your pancakes or Yorkshire pudding, put in a dessertspoon "ATORA" (for pancakes), but for Yorkshire pudding add a tablespoon to each $\frac{1}{2}$ pint milk. This gives an excellent flavour, and will help to keep pancakes from sticking when being cooked.

TO TREAT A COUGH

A teaspoon of "ATORA", taken in a glass of hot milk at bed-time is a very soothing and beneficial treatment in the case of a cough or sore throat.

In the same way "ATORA" is definitely beneficial in all cases of catarrh, chest or bronchial troubles, and should be taken regularly in hot milk as indicated.

ALL RECIPES THROUGHOUT THE BOOK ARE SUFFICIENT FOR FOUR AVERAGE PORTIONS

---

lise under controlled conditions, mixing it with flour and extruding it to the specified shape and length. By so doing, he created a shredded form of suet which could be kept for long periods in the kitchen cupboard at ambient temperature and which was much easier to handle and mix than many other fats such as dripping, lard or butter. The old Atora recipe books make many exaggerated claims about the life-enhancing properties of suet (see above), which in today's health-conscious age would invite immediate litigation.

Nevertheless, demand for Atora had remained remarkably robust, supported by a very effective category marketing approach by McDougall's Foods Ltd, the RHM company latterly responsible for the brand. They had worked creatively with the retailers to drive sales of Atora, particularly at the expense of the retailers' private label suet lines, while the development of a vegetarian suet line, Atora Light, had bolstered and widened the product's appeal. The gradual decline in the nation's consumption of products made

with suet such as jam roly-poly, steak and kidney pudding and, to a lesser extent, mincemeat, had resulted in a corresponding decline in the overall demand for suet, but by ensuring that the Atora brand became and remained virtually synonymous with suet, the McDougall's Foods team had created a very profitable and robust cash generator for RHM. The move to Ledbury led to an immediate increase in the profitability of the brand as a result of lower production costs. More importantly, it paved the way within just over three years to an eventual doubling of output and a consolidation of RHM's market leadership which would underwrite the brand's profitability for years to come.

David Smith had initially seen the opportunity to extend Atora into the ingredient sector. Neither Centura, McDougall's nor RHM Foods before them had had any great interest in, or feeling for, the ingredients market. The Ledbury Preserves business, in contrast, had been having great success with a targeted strategy aimed at industrial bakeries and other food manufacturers. Smith proposed a strategy aimed at selling suet alongside industrial preserves and he found a keen ally when Ken Jollans succeeded Dean Holroyd as managing director in late 2002. Although there would initially appear to be little commonality between preserves and suet, in fact a number of Ledbury customers (and oddly Robertson's-Ledbury Preserves itself!) purchased bulk suet from a competitor, Broadland Foods, typically for use in mincemeat and sweet puddings. Additionally many producers of savoury ready meals used bulk suet in their recipes.

Broadland Foods was the only real competitor. It had been acquired some years previously as part of a larger transaction by Danisco, a Danish company focused primarily on niche and high value food ingredients with a worldwide customer base. Danisco had initially left Broadland to go its own way, but the success of Atora in the retail sector had left the company overdependent on the industrial suet market. When Smith's strategy of targeting this market with suet from Ledbury started to have an impact, Danisco concluded that there was no real room for two large scale suet producers and started the process which led in early 2006 to the closure of the Broadland factory in Birmingham. A mechanism was agreed which benefited both Danisco and RHM by arranging for an orderly exit for Broadland and a smooth transfer of customers to Ledbury. The financial benefits, both direct and indirect, for the Ledbury business were considerable and helped to underwrite the company's profit growth in both 2005-6 and 2006-7.

The success of the commercial strategy almost caught the production team on the hop. Although the value of the Broadland suet business was much less than that of RHM, the volume was broadly similar. By the time the Birmingham factory closed in early 2006, that winter's seasonal peak was almost over and this induced a mistaken sense of security. When the whole nation's peak retail and industrial demand hit Ledbury in late 2006 and early 2007, the factory could barely cope and there was a real threat of a nationwide suet shortage! The following year, steps were taken to ensure that sufficient stocks were built up during the low season to be better able to cope when peak demand hit.

11 ⌁ A Hidden Jewel

The Creation of Robertson's-Ledbury Preserves

As one half of James Robertson & Sons during the mid nineties, the Ledbury business became more and more specialised. While the sister operation in Droylsden concentrated increasingly on the efficient production and mass marketing of the well known Robertson's, Golden Shred and Frank Cooper brands, Ledbury grew primarily by focusing on high quality 'private label' retail and bespoke industrial preserves. The established and strong relationships with Marks & Spencer and the various RHM cake bakeries continued to underpin the business but Ledbury also supplied significant volumes of fresh fruit marmalade and high quality conserves in particular to Tesco and Sainsbury's throughout this period.

Sales to a number of other major cake and biscuit manufacturers also continued to grow. As the company built up its reputation as a market leading supplier of industrial preserves, it was able steadily to pick and choose which sectors of this market it wanted to target. David Smith's commercial strategy was  to leave the 'red sticky stuff' to the competitors and to develop sales of specialised and higher value products particularly to the stronger branded businesses including Burton's, Fox's and McVitie's. At the same time, the focus on cost control which was a hallmark of the Tomkins regime ensured that much of the increased revenue dropped straight through to the profit line. Slowly but surely, the Ledbury business became the most profitable half of the James Robertson business, to the surprise of many people both within and outside the business. Paul Wilkinson, chairman of RHM, was wont to refer to Ledbury as the group's 'hidden jewel'.

When RHM decided in 1999 to carry out another corporate reorganisation, it was time for the Ledbury business to stand on its own feet again. The Droylsden operation was subsumed into the new Centura Foods division, which brought together RHM's main grocery brands including Sharwoods

and Bisto alongside Robertson's and the other preserves brands. Robertson's-Ledbury Preserves Ltd came into being and took its place in RHM's new Food Ingredients Division, recognising the growing predominance of the industrial business stream. The new name was something of a compromise. It successfully, if possibly superfluously, retained the cachet of the Robertson's name but for years to come this would cause confusion in the outside world, particularly since there was no longer any other jam business trading under the Robertson's name. Regular requests would be received for golly memorabilia or for details of local suppliers of Golden Shred in various far corners of the globe.

Continued Growth

As a standalone business within RHM, the pressure was on the Ledbury management to deliver continued growth in sales, profit and return on capital. This pressure continued unabated when Tomkins sold RHM to a new owner from the world of private equity, Doughty Hanson, in 2000. The local management and workforce responded well and profit growth continued each year almost unabated right through until 2007. Managing Director Dean Holroyd moved on to a new challenge in RHM's Bakery division in 2002 and was replaced by Ken Jollans, who remained in the role until the end of our story.

Dean Holroyd

Ken Jollans

The performance of the company during the early years of the new millennium was even more creditable when viewed in the light of the simultaneous tribulations experienced by some of the companies whose success had helped provide such a platform for growth in the nineties, including Marks & Spencer and Manor Bakeries. After an extraordinarily successful and sustained period of growth, Marks & Spencer lost its way and sales declined. This was exacerbated by the dramatic decision by the retailer in 2001 to close all its stores in mainland Europe. Many of these shops, particularly in France, had sold large volumes of marmalade and the almost overnight loss of this revenue, coupled with the simultaneous underperformance of M&S's UK stores, hit the Ledbury business hard. The following year saw the loss of the Sainsbury's conserve contract, which had been supplied from Ledbury for many years. During this period, the sales responsibilities for all retailers except M&S were handled by Centura. This relationship didn't do Ledbury any favours. The Centura team was much more interested in selling its own profitable branded products than in helping Ledbury to sell private label products with a shared profit margin. Despite this, however, the loss of the Sainsbury business was also a reflection of economic reality, with a number of large, efficient and aggressive continental preserves manufacturers able and willing to offer mass market but nevertheless good quality conserves to the major UK retailers at increasingly competitive prices. Ledbury simply didn't have the scale to be able to fight back. Instead, the business kept on focusing on those areas where it had a unique selling proposition, in industrial preserves, fresh fruit marmalades and high quality private label conserves. The introduction of suet production in 2002 and the transfer of all of RHM's retail mincemeat production to Ledbury in 2005 added two further areas of specialisation and potential for growth.

The story of how Ledbury came to supply the world's suet has been told in Chapter 10. The introduction of Robertson's mincemeat had a similar background in so far as it allowed RHM to make significant savings by closing the inefficient and virtually obsolete mincemeat plant in Droylsden. A new production unit was sited in the old 'Dorset' area. Capital expenditure for the project was restricted and compromises were made which meant that production never became as efficient or reliable as had been intended, but the impulse of extra volume gave Ledbury a real critical mass and leading presence in the market for retail as well as industrial mincemeat.

Creating a Platform for the Future . . .

A benefit of being a standalone business within RHM was that the business was required to have a self-reliant management team with functional expertise across the business. Decision making became quick and informed and what the business may have missed in terms of formal processes, it more than made up for by its ability to think and act quickly and to provide customers with a joined up approach, tailored to meet their individual requirements. Customers weren't just left to the sales team to deal with; where it was appropriate, they worked also in close partnership with the technical, operational and financial departments. The business started to invest for the first time in the development and training of its managers and team leaders and for the first time, a human resources manager was appointed. This was additionally important because it was becoming harder to recruit skilled and reliable staff to the business, as the local economy grew and as the demographic make-up of the town of Ledbury started to change. This situation changed following the accession of ten new countries to the European Union in 2004. The business eventually recruited a number of Eastern European employees on both temporary and permanent contracts and factory notices started to appear in Polish as well as in English. There was a certain irony when some of the fruit price rises experienced by the business in 2007 were put down to a shortage of manpower in Poland to pick the fruit!

Success brings its own challenges and the pressure to find new growth opportunities continued. The introduction of Atora and the Centura mincemeat business had complemented the continued growth of sales in industrial preserves but this couldn't disguise the fact that core retail sales were in long-term decline. An earlier attempt to employ a dedicated retail sales manager had foundered and the limitations of the restrictive relationship with Centura, who retained primary responsibility for sales to all retail customers with the exception of M&S, were causing much frustration. Robertson's-Ledbury Preserves was able to produce some of the best preserves in the world but didn't have the resources to be able to sell or market them; something had to change. In 2005, the company took the bold step of virtually doubling the sales budget and increasing the size of the sales team by three, including a new commercial director, Dominic Shaw, who had been the Ledbury technical manager a decade earlier. A new retail sales manager was recruited from Centura and put onto the Ledbury payroll with the express aim of sponsoring and developing new sales opportunities

A POLISH VIEWPOINT

Herefordshire isn't the most multi-ethnic of counties and for most of its history, even allowing for the impact of the Hungarian Imric Jagan and latterly the Dutchman Willem van Meeuwen, foreign or immigrant employees have been few and far between. This changed in the last few years of operation when Eastern European temporary workers were employed in considerable numbers to meet short-term peaks in demand. One of the first to be taken onto the payroll as a permanent employee was Piotr Falicki, who came to the area in February 2005 from a small town in north-west Poland, where he had worked for six years as a travel agent.

He and three friends had been recruited in Poland by the Polish-born foreman of a Herefordshire fruit farm. The level of wages and living conditions were very poor: twelve hour shifts, six days a week for £250 a month, living in caravans. In due course, he got temporary work at Ledbury Preserves. He spent eight months doing warehouse and stacking work but was tantalised by the sweet smells coming from the factory. He finally obtained a permanent position making toffee and fruit fillings, but found this boring work. Later, he got involved in the citrus processing which, while mentally undemanding, at least involved physical activity. He described the factory as a happy place to work.

Piotr spoke little English when he arrived and he accepted that fruit picking and factory work was all that he could expect initially. However, he learnt a lot of English, entirely by conversation without going to classes. One of the young men who came with him had been good at English at school but found himself unable to say a word to anyone when he got here, and soon went home; Piotr found it easier to dive in and listen and converse without any formal teaching.

Alongside his work in the jam factory, he also took on a lot of odd jobs, including painting, decorating and tiling. He describes himself as a 'handyman' (which he thinks is a very funny word). His wife and young son came to join him after eighteen months. His son spoke no English at all and the first few months were hard but he soon started chattering away and enjoying school. His wife, who also worked in the factory, found it more difficult to learn English. They have enjoyed living in Ledbury, which they see as a 'quiet, safe town'. They have found the English to be much more open and welcoming than they had expected. They like to explore when they can. In fact, when he was first here with his friends, they bought a car and travelled about as much as they could, doing everything from Alton Towers to Stonehenge and visiting London. He has been surprised to meet people in Ledbury who have never been to London.

with the multiple retailers. The increased focus paid early dividends with the first new Ledbury products for some years being developed for Tesco and Sainsbury among others. As a result, and along with the introduction of two major new contracts during 2007, the D Section filling line reached effective capacity for the first time for many years.

Shaw's return solved a problem which had been a headache for Jollans for some time. He brought with him a strong combination of commercial and technical experience in both the retail and food ingredient sectors, which fitted well with the specific and unusual customer and product portfolio of the Ledbury business. Crucially, it allowed David Smith to step out of the front line, although he continued to support the business in a consultancy role. Smith's contribution to the business over more than three decades had been of considerable importance and it is indeed questionable whether the Ledbury factory would have survived as long as it did without him. Nominally, he only worked part-time, combining his life in jam with a prominent role in the Pioneer Ministry of the Jehovah's Witnesses, but he retained a huge involvement in, and enthusiasm for, the Ledbury business which belied any suggestion that his business focus might suffer from divided loyalties.

David Smith

Despite the company's strong financial performance, funds for capital investment remained tight. Tomkins had had very strict criteria with regard to the required rate of return on capital expenditure, and this didn't get any easier under Doughty Hanson or following RHM's return to the London Stock Exchange in 2005. The capital which was available tended to be for major one-off projects, such as the introduction of suet in 2002 and Centura mincemeat in 2005, or in the area of regulatory compliance such as the new effluent processing plant which was opened by the mayor of Ledbury in 2004. Relatively little money was ever spent on upgrading the site infrastructure.

In October 2006, the Ledbury management presented a radical new plan to RHM, with the proposal to merge the jam operations in Droylsden and Ledbury onto one site. Agreement was reached with the RHM Culinary Brands Division, which had subsumed Centura, to carry out a review of options and to include a detailed proposal in the budget for 2007-8. The review of options was expected to have only one likely outcome, not least because the proximity of the new M60 motorway meant that the Droylsden site had now become a valuable piece of real estate with considerable development potential. But the tectonic plates were shifting. RHM's share

The Mayor of Ledbury opens the new effluent plant on 14 March 2005

performance had been lack-lustre ever since the group had issued what was widely interpreted as a profits warning within six months of the flotation in the previous year. On 4 December 2006, Premier Foods announced an agreed takeover of RHM and suddenly all bets were off.

Richard Moore was the preserves production manager during the jam factory's final years. He began in 1983 stacking, but within a week he was recruited into the boiling area. When the factory moved on to shifts, he became a chargehand.

In those days, the factory was chaotic. Production was not very mechanised and there were a lot of staff. Work wasn't well planned and it was a regular occurrence for employees on the early shift to be told by their manager as they were about to go home that they were needed for the evening shift as well. Some employees used this chaos to their advantage, working Monday to Thursday, getting overtime, then taking Friday off and being paid the same amount of money.

Richard's father was a chargehand in the engineering department and he can remember his father once falling in a tank of jam. He had been standing on a tank to change a light fitting and had to go to the engineering workshop for a new switch. When he came back, the tank had been replaced by another. He jumped up and fell right in the different-sized tank.

Richard recalls it being a relaxed factory in his early days. Even later, at the very end, he remarked that you wouldn't think it was closing because the attitude of the staff never changed. People always helped one another. If there was a problem, people were always there to there to lend a hand.

12 ⁓ A Sticky End

A New Parent

RHM's return to the London Stock Exchange in 2005 had been very lucrative for Doughty Hanson and its investors. However, the City retained a certain scepticism about the group's strategy and direction, which was only encouraged by the profits warning in October of that year, caused primarily by continuing difficulties at Manor Bakeries. The share price drifted and investor frustration grew as a series of perceived acquisition opportunities went begging, with rival Premier Foods repeatedly outbidding RHM, notably in the auction for the Campbell's UK business in 2006. In contrast to RHM, Premier was seen by the investor community as dynamic, successful and strategically farsighted. When Premier came knocking at the door in the autumn of 2006 with a bid worth 30 per cent more than the share price at the time, it didn't take the RHM board long to agree to recommend acceptance.

The two businesses fitted well together. Each owned a stable of traditional UK ambient grocery brands with relatively little overlap. One of the few areas where the two businesses went head to head was in preserves, with Premier owning the Hartley's and Rose's brands as well as having a significant volume business in industrial preserves. The Office of Fair Trading looked briefly at the impact which the acquisition would have on market balance but decided not to refer it to the Competition Commission. On 15 March 2007, the takeover took effect and Robertson's-Ledbury Preserves became part of Premier Foods Plc.

Writing on the Wall

As soon as news of the deal had broken, there were concerns among the workforce about the future of the site, in the knowledge that Premier and RHM between them had three jam factories (to which a fourth would soon be added with the acquisition of Chivers Ireland). It was hoped locally that Ledbury's strength as a specialist and profitable niche business, boosted by the success of the suet operation, could see it survive although the shape of the business would inevitably change. However, in retrospect, the writing was on the wall as soon as the RHM Board had accepted Premier's bid. In order to satisfy their own investors, Premier had to move fast to demonstrate that the £85m of annual synergy benefits which they had promised were realistic. In contrast to RHM, Premier operated a streamlined and centralised business, with little room for the type of specialisation and differentiation which characterised the Ledbury operation. The heartland of Premier's business was centred around a small number of big factories producing ambient grocery products in East Anglia, most of which were already in the process of taking on additional volume as a result of the factory rationalisation programme following the Campbells acquisition. Right from the start, Premier intended to continue this programme of making the big factories bigger by closing a number of smaller RHM sites, including both Ledbury and Droylsden.

Within weeks of the takeover, a manufacturing review codenamed 'Project Margaret' was announced. Senior operational managers from all the ambient grocery factories in the new combined business took part in this review, including Ken Jollans on behalf of Ledbury. The core manufacturing principles of Premier Foods provided the context within which the review was carried out. These principles placed great emphasis on scale and efficiency. On 2 July 2007, only fifteen weeks after completion of the Premier takeover, Jollans called the workforce together in the canteen and read out a prepared statement which confirmed that the factory would close during 2008, along with five other ex-RHM sites. All the Ledbury production was to be transferred to the Premier factory in Histon, Cambridgeshire.

Although most employees understood that the outcome of the manufacturing review would have implications for Ledbury, few expected a complete factory closure to be announced. Many of the people at the meeting had spent most of their career at the factory and took pride in having been part of a strong and growing business, particularly in the last decade. But in the following days, as the workforce and the town started to come to terms with the news, they showed their character. To a man and woman, the workers reacted with great dignity, conscientiously getting on with their jobs and displaying considerable discipline and maturity both when being 'doorstepped' by regional news reporters and in the briefings and consultation meetings which followed the closure announcement.

Factory closure by autumn 2008

From the Ledbury Reporter, first published Friday 6th Jul 2007.

PREMIER Foods is set to close Robertson's Ledbury Preserves by the autumn of 2008 and shift manufacture of the plant's products to Cambridgeshire.

The 177-strong workforce was told the news on Monday but have been forbidden to speak to the press.

In a statement, Premier Foods said: "After careful consideration of 11 overlapping sites, the company has announced consultation on proposals to restructure some of its manufacturing sites, which would mean the closure of the Ledbury site by September 2008.

"Products currently manufactured at the site, including Robertson's jam, suet and mincemeat, will transfer to Histon in Cambridgeshire."

Chief executive Robert Schofield said: "We understand the impact that these proposals will have on the individuals directly affected and we will work with them to explore opportunities for redeployment within the group and elsewhere."

David Smith, who was the commercial manager at the site until last year, said: "Many of those at Ledbury Preserves may be third or fourth generation among local families to work there and it is those that I particularly feel for. I think my concerns are for those who are older, for the obvious reasons.

"It is a sad thing that, despite success, vision, technology and excellence, economic demands bring us to this day."

A Reprieve for Suet

The speed with which Premier had taken the decision to close six RHM factories was indicative of a dynamic organisation with the wind in its sails, but the truth was that many details of the plan were sketchy if not flaky and before the year was out, the plan would be changed considerably. An early indication of challenges ahead had come when Marks & Spencer reacted frostily to having been informed only a few days before the announcement of the plan to close Ledbury. A number of Ledbury managers with strong relationships at the M&S head office at Waterside in London went further than the call of duty in sponsoring and supporting the transfer process and after a scare or two, M&S came on board.

By this stage, it was clear that the original plans for Histon to accommodate the Ledbury and Droylsden volume were not going to work. The first plan for suet was to take over a part of the Histon warehouse, but the limitations of this plan were soon exposed and an alternative plan was developed. This plan killed two birds with one stone, since it involved the outsourcing of peanut butter production, enabling the site to become 'nut free' (an M&S requirement), which freed up a building in a good state of repair to use for suet production. However, this plan itself was challenged almost as soon as it had been drawn up, as it quickly became clear that the buildings initially earmarked for M&S production were not going to meet the retailer's requirements without a great deal of expenditure. The peanut butter building provided the ideal solution . . . but what about suet?

In October 2007, Premier started to market the Ledbury site, amounting to 28 acres in total, with the intention of agreeing a sale and leaseback before the end of the year. By this stage, some of Premier's more fanciful ideas as to the value of the site had been tempered. A local businessman, David Hepworth, was interested in the site for apple milling and drink manufacture. In passing, he also expressed a readiness to continue suet manufacturing on Premier's behalf. Negotiations moved quickly and on 21 December 2007, the site was sold to Universal Beverages Ltd, a joint venture between Scottish & Newcastle Breweries Plc and Hepworth's Q Group. At the same time, a contract for an initial period of three years was signed for the new owners to produce suet at Ledbury for Premier Foods. Locally, 20 jobs had been saved and many more would be created by the new venture, but there would no longer be any jam production on Little Marcle Road.

Along with these and other changes to the original plans, Premier also took the opportunity of the 'Project Margaret' integration and rationalisation programme to review and trim the number of 'stock keeping units' (SKUs) in the joint portfolio. In Ledbury's case, this particularly focused on the industrial preserves product range. There was some genuine, albeit limited, overlap between the industrial product ranges of Histon and Ledbury, but there was also a considerable philosophical difference in the way the two old competitors had handled new product development and product differentiation. For some years, Ledbury—as a specialist supplier of bakery jams in particular—had pursued a policy of specialisation and associated price and margin improvement. By contrast, Histon saw industrial preserves as a non-core cash generator. They had a much more restricted product portfolio with much lower prices and margins. Both strategies were valid and both had been successful, but it was clearly not going to be easy to make them compatible in the new context. The SKU rationalisation process made clear sense from the Premier standpoint and had the benefit of significantly simplifying the product matching and product transfer process prior to the Ledbury closure. But whether the Ledbury business would remain recognisable following the Histon transfer and the simultaneous SKU rationalisation was, to say the least, moot.

ACKNOWLEDGEMENTS

This book has been written and produced by a dedicated team of people acting largely on a voluntary basis and, in many cases, going far beyond any call of duty to ensure that its publication coincided with the final closure of The Pozzy. Brian Hudson launched himself into the project with verve and authority and unearthed much more about the early years of the business than we had ever anticipated. David Smith agreed originally to draft three chapters but ended up writing six, applying the great knowledge and experience he gained from working as a senior manager of the business for over three decades and combining this with a sharp intellect, a keen eye for detail and a light touch. Guy Malkerson gave valuable advice and support in transforming our pages of word-processing into a published book, in addition to which, he carried out a number of interviews with long serving employees which provided valuable material for the later chapters and which he recorded with a lyrical flair which will be immediately recognisable. Gill Blakeley worked tirelessly to pull it all together and to ensure that it all happened on time and within budget. Dr Sylvia Pinches carried out valuable research relating to the very early history and pointed us in a number of right directions. Judy Hooley showed continuing enthusiasm and fostered the co-operation between the company and the local historians which has been at the heart of the project.

Many current and ex-employees contributed greatly by recalling and sharing their memories and producing many wonderful old photos. It was a repeated joy to hear so many people talk with great affection about happy times at The Pozzy and to learn that it was always much more than a place of work. We also spoke with suppliers, customers, neighbours and competitors along the way. We would like to thank the following people for their help and support:

Doreen Bailey, Lyn Ballard, Rosemary Ballard, Tom Barrett, Peggy Beach, Christine Bebbington, Margaret Bradstock, Dudley Brook, Steve Bunn, Brian Callan, Roger Callan, Allan Clarke, Beryl Davenport, Les Davenport, Wendy Diment, Ruth Edwards, Norman Edwards, Piotr Falicki, Stan George, Ann Gladwin, Gerald Hanford, Lil Hopkins, Dave Jones, Monica

Jones, Gill Kitching, John Kitching, Ginny Knox, Frances Lawrence, Kate Loxton, Melvyn Manns, Keith Manson, Mike McQuaid, John Mitchell, Richard Moore, Violet Mowberry, Peter Owen-Ward, Bill Pearce, Jan Pearce, Mark Phelan, Margaret Phillips, Roy Poole, Dr John Randall, Annie Roberts, Dominic Shaw, Dave Sturge, Polly Sturge, Edward Thompson and Ian Wheeler.

Brian Callan, in particular, went far beyond the call of duty and did much invaluable research without which this book would have been very much the poorer. We also acknowledge the research work carried out by Andrew Romanowski and Bill Turberfield. Kirsty Shields of Marks & Spencer unearthed valuable archive information after much digging. Jennifer Whittington drew a number of sketches with admirable accuracy, never having actually seen her subjects face to face.

Publication of the book on an independent basis was made financially possible as a result of generous support from a number of sponsors including many long-standing suppliers. We thank the following businesses and wish them all well in their future dealings with Premier Foods:

AarhusKarlshamn UK Ltd, ABE Ledbury Ltd, Ardagh Glass, Atchison Topeka Transport, J Fulton & Co, Greencell Ltd, H E Stringer Ltd, Overseal Natural Ingredients, Place UK Ltd, D S Smith Packaging, Zest Catering Solutions

I would finally like to thank Premier Foods Plc for its generous and indulgent support.

Ken Jollans